# QUAQTAQ: MODERNITY AND IDENTITY IN AN INUIT COMMUNITY

How, in a world that is drastically changing, can the Inuit preserve their identity? Louis-Jacques Dorais explores this question in *Quaqtaq*, the first ethnography of a contemporary Canadian Inuit community to be published in over twenty-five years. The community of Quaqtaq is a small village on Hudson Strait where hunting and gathering are still the mainstays of life. In this description of Quaqtaq, based on data collected over a thirty-year period, we get a glimpse of its early cultural history, its development into a settled community, and its present realities. Dorais identifies three principal manifestations of local identity – kinship, religion, and language – that persist despite the brutal intrusion of modernity. He concludes by examining the role politics and education have played in the relationship between Quaqtaq and the outside world. *Quaqtaq* is a unique and important study that will be of interest to scholars, administrators, and citizens of Inuit and other native communities.

LOUIS-JACQUES DORAIS is Professor of Anthropology, Université Laval, and is editor of *Études/Inuit/Studies*.

LOUIS-JACQUES DORAIS

# Quaqtaq:
# Modernity and Identity in an
# Inuit Community

UNIVERSITY OF TORONTO PRESS
Toronto Buffalo London

© University of Toronto Press Incorporated 1997
Toronto Buffalo London
Printed in Canada

Reprinted 2001

ISBN 0-8020-4105-1 (cloth)
ISBN 0-8020-7952-0 (paper)

Printed on acid-free paper

---

**Canadian Cataloguing in Publication Data**

Dorais, Louis-Jacques, 1945–
  Quaqtaq

  Includes bibliographical references and index.
  ISBN 0-8020-4105-1 (bound)
  ISBN 0-8020-7952-0 (pbk.)

  1. Inuit – Cultural assimilation – Quebec (Province) –
  Quaqtaq.   2. Inuit – Quebec (Province) – Quaqtaq –
  Ethnic identity.   3. Inuit – Quebec (Province) – Quaqtaq –
  Social conditions.   4. Inuit – Quebec (Province) –
  Quaqtaq – Social life and customs.   I. Title.

  E99.E7D665 1997   306′.0899710714111   C96-932195-3

---

University of Toronto Press acknowledges the financial assistance to its publishing
program of the Canada Council and the Ontario Arts Council.

This book has been published with the help of a grant from the Humanities and
Social Sciences Federation of Canada, using funds provided by the Social Sciences
and Humanities Research Council of Canada.

University of Toronto Press acknowledges the financial support for its publishing activities of the Government of Canada through the Book Publishing
Industry Development Program (BPIDP).

# Contents

relie on lectures

focus on this

# Preface

I first set foot in Quaqtaq on 26 May 1965, arriving by snowmobile from the neighbouring village of Kangirsuk. It was early spring. During the day the thermometer rose over the freezing point, but at night it still stood well below it. The sea and lake ice had not started melting yet, although on land the snow cover was slowly beginning to disappear.

I was an anthropology student from Université de Montréal, anxious to experience contact with a culture that I imagined to be totally different from my own, and, quite secondarily, eager to collect data for my master's thesis. My first stay in the village, and in the nearby hunting camp of Airartuuq, lasted till the end of August. I lived part of my time with an Inuit family, trying to participate as well as I could in the daily activities of the community (told in Dorais 1985). The story repeated itself the next summer (May to September 1966), and during the Christmas season (December 1966 to January 1967). By then, I had learned the language, Inuktitut, and was in a better position to inquire about various aspects of local history, economy, and social life in general. I had also established firm friendships among the Quaqtamiut (the people of Quaqtaq).

I spent a couple of days in the village in July 1968, and about three weeks during summer 1969. I was gathering data – all around Nunavik (Arctic Quebec) – for my doctoral dissertation, which was to deal with the semantics of Inuit words designating newly introduced elements of the material culture. The completion of my doctoral degree (in Paris, France), a teaching job at Quebec City's Université Laval, marriage, and paternity then kept me away from Quaqtaq (but not from other Inuit communities) for many years. It was only in July 1981 that I had the opportunity to return in order to update (and later publish, Dorais 1984) my master's thesis on the social and economic development of the community.

In the meantime, I had not lost contact with the Quaqtamiut. The introduction of airplanes and telephones in the North, ranked among the more positive effects of modernity, enabled me to keep in touch, over the years, with those Quaqtaq residents who travelled or phoned *taununga qallunaanut* ('to down there among the Qallunaat [White people]').

In the early 1990s, my participation in a research project concerned with the role played by education in shaping contemporary Inuit culture and identity enabled me to visit Quaqtaq twice again, in May–June 1990 and March 1993. My inquiries on these trips were more specifically aimed at defining what it meant to be an Inuk, and a Quaqtamiuq, at the end of the twentieth century. I was also eager to assess the development of the community since my first stay there.

This book is the outcome of my twenty-eight years of contact with Quaqtaq. Its completion would have been imposssible if the community's residents had not offered me their friendship and, I think, their trust. They may not totally agree with my interpretation of their culture, but they should know that I always tried to approach it with the utmost care and respect. Any factual or interpretative error is due to my own shortcomings, and not to any desire to bear a judgment on them.

I thus wish to thank warmly all the Quaqtamiut who welcomed me to their community. Most of them are still alive. Those who have died since my first visit live again, in a way, through those who now bear their names. Special thanks must go to my adoptive Inuit parents, Charlie and Mary Tukkiapik (Taqqiapik), who over the years genuinely considered me their *irniq* (son): *nakurmimarialungai ataata, anaana, ikajuqattalaurattik.* I also wish to thank David Okpik (Uppik), the only English-speaking adult Quaqtamiuq back in 1965, oftentimes mayor of Quaqtaq, and a noted movie star. Thanks are due also to Eva Kiliutaq-Deer, principal of the community school and mayor of the village, and to Lizzie Ningiuruvik who, with Okpik and Kiliutaq-Deer, read a draft version of this book and sent me useful comments.

Other people and organizations deserve my gratitude. My fieldwork would have been much more difficult to undertake without the logistical support and moral encouragement of Fathers Joseph Meeus, Ernest Trinel, Robert Lechat, and Lucien Schneider, O.M.I., former missionaries to Quaqtaq and Kuujjuaq, and of Orville Cassidy, David Wiebe, and Jean-Paul Matte, respectively federal teachers and Quebec governmental agent in Quaqtaq, in 1965–7. On the intellectual side, my master's thesis advisers, Professors Rémi Savard, Asen Balikci, and Bernard Saladin d'Anglure, instilled in me a passion for Inuit culture, language, and society that has not yet met its end. Bernard Saladin (Pirnaaluk) in particular, who later became a colleague and friend, introduced me to northern fieldwork and always encouraged my efforts to better understand the Inuit ways. Anthropologists William B. Kemp (Pupualuk) and Nelson H.H. Graburn (Kajuk), who visited Quaqtaq shortly before my first stay there, shared some interesting ideas about the ethnohistory of the community. More recently, my reflection on Inuit identity greatly benefited from discussions with Drs. Susanne Dybbroe, Poul Møller, Pierre and Bernadette Robbe, Susan Sammons, Arlene Stairs, and George Wenzel, and from the comments of the three anonymous referees who read my draft manuscript of this book.

Last but not least, I must thank all the organizations which, over the past thirty years, made my fieldwork – and this publication – possible: Canada's Department of Indian and Northern Affairs, Quebec's Ministère des Affaires culturelles, Université Laval's Centre d'études nordiques, the Social Sciences and Humanities Research Council of Canada (formerly the Canada Council), and the Aid to Scholarly Publications Programme of the Humanities and Social Sciences Federation of Canada. Some passages from the present book are inspired by my previous study on Quaqtaq's history (Dorais 1984). They are used here with permission from the original publisher, Recherches amérindiennes au Québec. The maps and genealogical material were drawn by Johanne Levesque.

Throughout the text, words in Inuktitut are written in the Nunavik version of Inuit Tapirisat of Canada's standard Roman orthography, where the letter q is a uvular stop (pronounced 'kr'), and aa, ii, and uu are long vowels.

Abandoned cabin on the site of the former trading posts, Iggiajaq (Diana Bay), August 1966

Nuvuk (Cape Hopes Advance), the site of the weather station, August 1966

Ilaijja's tent at spring camp of Illutalik, June 1966 (note the frozen expanse of Tuvaaluk)

Part of the village of Quaqtaq, June 1966

Seaside area of Quaqtaq, August 1966

A dogteam is ready to leave for the spring camp, Quaqtaq, June 1966

Jaani fishing through the sea ice, Siaqqituuq, June 1966

Saali getting his screen ready for approaching *uuttuit* (seal basking on the sea ice), Tuvaaluk, June 1966

Saali waiting for seal at Airartuuq, July 1966

Saali flensing the seal he just caught, Airartuuq, July 1966

Inugaluaq and Miaji flensing a beluga, Quaqtaq, July 1966

Matiusi's Perterhead boat, Quaqtaq, August 1966

Jaani in his canoe near Iqaluppilik, August 1966

Tivi untangling his fishing net, Iqaluppilik, August 1966

Saali at home with his daughter Tisi, Quaqtaq, June 1966

Delivering oil to a private residence, Quaqtaq, June 1990

The cooperative store, Quaqtaq, June 1990

# QUAQTAQ: MODERNITY AND IDENTITY IN AN INUIT COMMUNITY

# Introduction:
# On Modernity, Identity, and Quaqtaq

Quaqtaq is a small predominantly Inuit village in Nunavik (Arctic Quebec). In 1990 the village had 225 residents. Like all other native communities in the Canadian North, Quaqtaq has experienced, and is still experiencing, tremendous change. As anywhere else in the Arctic, present-day life there has almost nothing in common with what it used to be seventy, fifty, or even thirty years ago. The nomadic igloo-dwellers of the Qallunaat's (white people) fantasies have become sedentary wage workers and/or sophisticated harvesters of faunal resources. Inuit society, in many respects, is as modern as its Euro-American counterpart.

Inuit, however, continue to consider themselves to be Inuit. In spite of cultural and social change, they feel strong continuity between their past and present. Many born and raised on the land now occupy key economic, political, managerial, and educational positions within an administrative apparatus that did not even exist twenty-five years ago. But these people, and most of their fellow Inuit, do not perceive any major break in their personal identity. They accept change as it comes, and modifications in their lifestyle and cultural habits do not alter their individuality. Their social and natural environments may have been transformed, but they still try to relate to them as fully as possible. Even young Quaqtamiut, who are likely to perceive major differences between themselves and their parents (and vice versa), generally are able to establish functional and meaningful social relations with their elders.

Thus, in Quaqtaq, as elsewhere in the North, modernity and identity constantly interact. In this book I propose to depict this interaction. Chapters on the cultural and social history of the community will be followed by a description of contemporary Quaqtaq and by an account of its residents' identity and relationship with the outside world. A short conclusion will address the question: Can one be at the same time Inuk and modern?

## Modernity

First, a few points must be made clear. This is not a treatise on modernity and identity. It is a description of the recent history and social life of a contemporary aboriginal community. The focus of this description is the question of identity, but no attempt is made to contribute to the advancement of theory on this topic, nor on modernity. The latter, for example, has been and often still is discussed by social scientists. Many anthropologists and sociologists currently debate the alleged modernity or postmodernity of the societies they study, wondering, for example, whether present-day hunting–gathering cultures may be considered modern, or whether European and North American postindustrial and post–Cold War societies have not reached a point that puts them beyond modernity.[1]

I do not intend to enter into this kind of discussion here. For the purposes of this book, modernity is defined as the more or less brutal inclusion of the Inuit into contemporary mainstream society. This inclusion forced on them economic, political, and cultural institutions (such as money, wage labour, government, Christianity, schools, and the mass media) suited, perhaps, to Western capitalist societies, but not necessarily reflecting aboriginal values and attitudes. According to specialists, such as Giddens (1991), modernity has four principal characteristics: (1) separation of space and time, (2) eradication of local values and attitudes, (3) reflexivity (the ability to reflect about one's own situation), and (4) standardization of symbols. As we shall see, most of these now seem to be at work among Inuit, who are losing control over their use of space and time,[2] and as for exogenous habits and ideas – including many standard North American cultural symbols – these were introduced to the Arctic a long time ago. Concerning reflexivity, a more or less stereotyped reflection on the aboriginal condition of the Arctic natives is being developed today by Inuit politicians and ethnic organizations.

Modernity also entails the advent of individualism (see Arcand 1993), as well as the perception of work as a specialized task, rather than as part of a total way of life. When modernity occurs in a society such as that of the Inuit, putting stress on both collective harmony and unity between the self and the environment, it is surely likely to provoke deep-reaching reactions and changes.[3]

## Identity

These changes may affect a person's or a group's identity, that is, the ways of doing, thinking, perceiving, and being perceived that make an individual or collectivity unique. Identity is often qualified. One speaks about cultural, social, or ethnic identity, or, to mix things a little, about sociocultural, ethnocultural, or ethnosocial identity.

Whatever its qualifications, however, identity *is not* simply the label (e.g., 'Inuit' or 'Qallunaat') affixed to a particular people, nor does it consist in a list of cultural traits defining the artefacts, behaviour, and world-view of a specific group of human beings. Identity is much more than that. According to various specialists on the subject (see for example, Barth 1969, Camilleri 1990, and Jacobson-Widding 1983), identity is a dynamic and creative process that is best expressed through the strategies developed to relate to one's physical, social, and spiritual environments. These environments may change over time and space, and thus identity is never fixed once and for all. It fluctuates constantly. An individual or a group may possess more than one identity – or develop varying relationships to the world – without losing his, her, or its sense of self.

For example, a male Inuk, whose main relationship to his territory and its animals, to his family and friends, and to Canadian society in general, used to be that of an Arctic hunter, may now primarily define himself as a politically and socially active member of his community, and of Nunavik in general, without feeling any break in his identity. He is still a man, bearer of one or several personal names, member of a family, dweller of a northern territory, and citizen of his village, region, and country. The sum of all these identities define him as Inuk.

Identity is thus a social and cultural construction. It includes various elements (such as sex, age, name, way of life, ideas, and language) that come together in a unique way within each individual (personal identity) or group (collective identity). This uniqueness is expressed through the strategic relationships that the individual or group maintains with the physical and spiritual environment and with other individuals and groups. These relationships are liable to change, and identity may transform itself very easily. This is a normal process, and it should not jeopardize one's sense of being unique and of belonging to a unique collectivity. A modern Inuk who works on a computer or teaches in a classroom is as much Inuk – if he or she perceives himself or herself as such – as is a traditional Inuk who spends his or her days hunting seals or sewing skin clothes.

Some people and organizations may assert the contrary. For them the only real Inuit are the traditional ones. People who make such assertions, however, generally do so because they find it in their interest to maintain a very conservative image of aboriginal peoples. Many Qallunaat would agree with granting cultural and linguistic rights to picturesque igloo-dwellers and hunters of wild game, but they are somewhat fearful of modern Inuit and Indians, who are claiming the economic and political rights of full-fledged nations. Similarly, to emphasize the differences between them and the rest of Canadian society, some Inuit organizations may deem it useful to depict their members as primarily preoccupied with traditional pursuits. In both cases, though, it is wrong to believe and let others believe that Inuit identity is bounded by a narrowly defined series of traditional cultural traits.

## Quaqtaq

Identity occurs within time, place, and a web of social relationships and cultural perceptions that all contribute to define it. The locus of occurrence that concerns us here, Quaqtaq (see Map 1), is a Nunavik community of 225 Inuit and 12 non-Inuit residents (in early 1993). The village (61°N. lat. by 69.40°W. long.) is located on the eastern shore of Tuvaaluk (Diana Bay), some 350 kilometres north of Kuujjuaq, the capital of Nunavik, and 1700 kilometres northeast of Montreal. Its nearest neighbours are the villages of Kangiqsujuaq (150 kilometres to the northwest, on Hudson Strait) and Kangirsuk (100 kilometres to the south, on Ungava Bay[4]). No roads connect Quaqtaq with the outside world.

Tuvaaluk (Map 2) is a middle-sized (thirty kilometres long) body of water that opens widely on Hudson Strait, the huge channel separating Quebec and Labrador from Baffin Island. Between Tuvaaluk and Ungava Bay, to the east, is a narrow (sixteen kilometres at its widest) and rather flat peninsula. From Quaqtaq it is thus very easy to travel across land and reach Ungava Bay, or to get to Nuvuk (Cape Hopes Advance), the northernmost tip of the peninsula (and, at some 125 metres, its highest summit), directly on Hudson Strait.

East and south of Tuvaaluk the landscape is characterized by low rocky hills. West of the bay, however, the hills are markedly higher and steeper, which makes northwestward travel by land more difficult. Both Tuvaaluk and the Ungava coast are dotted with numerous islands, most of them small, though one markedly larger island, Qikirtaaluk ('the big island'), lies in the northern half of Tuvaaluk, near its western shore.

Quaqtaq is situated well beyond the northern treeline. The only vegeta-

MAP 1
Nunavik (Arctic Quebec)

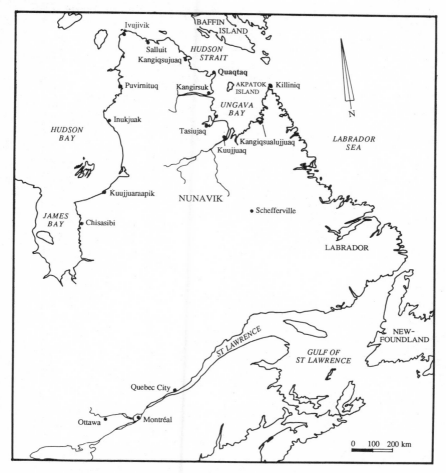

tion comprises lichens, small tundra flowers and berries,[5] dwarf birch, and, near ponds and rivers, high grass and (more rarely) willow bushes.

No large lakes or big rivers are found around Tuvaaluk, although four or five middle-sized bodies of water (one is three kilometres long) and a few streams, all favourable for fishing, lie south of the bay. Quaqtamiut also fish at Tasirjuakuluk (Robert's Lake), a large expanse of water about seventy kilometres south of Quaqtaq, towards Kangirsuk.

The Tuvaaluk region belongs to the Arctic. During July, the warmest

MAP 2
Tuvaaluk (Diana Bay)

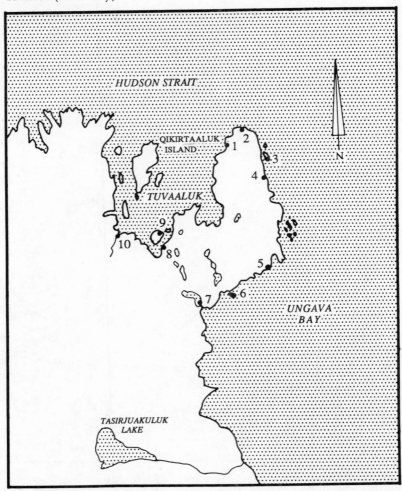

Principal Tuvaaluk Sites

1 Quaqtaq
2 Nuvuk
3 Airartuuq
4 Inutsulik
5 Imilik

6 Salliq
7 Iqaluppilik
8 Iggiajaq
9 Illutalik (Ipiutaq)
10 Siaqqituuq

month of the year, average temperatures do not exceed 10°C, although on sunny days, the thermometer may briefly reach 20°C. In January average temperatures hover around −20°C. The prevailing westerly winds contribute to the harshness of the climate.

Spring (*upirngasaaq*) begins in late May or early June, when the snow starts to melt and the rivers to thaw. It is only around 15 June, however, that contiguous sea ice (often called the floe) begins to break. The final dispersal of the last floating pans of sea ice, in late July, marks the start of summer (*upirngaaq*). Around 15 September, autumn (*ukiaq*) begins with the first snowfalls. The sea starts freezing over in October, and by the end of this month there is enough snow on the ground to enable travel by dog team and snowmobile. But full winter (*ukiuq*) only comes at the end of November, when, once again, the sea has turned to solid ice. Tuvaaluk is then entirely covered by solid ice, hence its name, 'the big expanse of ice.' Hudson Strait, however, because of the violence of sea currents, never completely freezes over. Pans of floating ice on it are carried on and away by the tides and winds.

Within Nunavik, the Tuvaaluk area is generally recognized as a kind of hunting paradise. The ringed (or common) seal (*natsiq; Phoca hispida*) is abundant year-round. In winter it comes breathing at the openings between the floating pans of ice or at the holes (*alluit*) it maintains in the floe, thanks to the warmth of its breath. In spring it often basks in the sun (*uuttuq*) on the sea ice. For a long time the staple food of Tuvaaluk Inuit was ringed seal meat.

The large bearded seal (*ujjuk; Erignathus barbatus*) is also found yearlong, but in smaller numbers. Its skin is very tough and can be used for making the soles of boots and leather thongs.

The harp or Greenland seal (*qairulik; Phoca groenlandica*) is rarely caught; it is generally found during spring and fall. The spotted (also called freshwater) seal (*qasigiaq; Phoca vitulina*) is also very infrequent; many hunters have never encountered it.

Until the 1970s the first walrus (*aiviq; Odobenus rosmarus*) herds of the year would reach the Ungava Bay coast in July, coming from Akpatok,[6] a huge island at the mouth of the bay, about eighty kilometres from its western shore. At the end of July and in early August they used to round Nuvuk in successive waves, swimming towards western Hudson Strait. They were seen again in November, on their way back to Akpatok. Nowadays, however, walruses have become a less frequent sight in the Tuvaaluk area.

The walrus would be preceded by beluga (*qilalugaq; Delphinapterus leucas*) herds, which also migrated in a northwesterly direction in June and

July and came back in October and November. These white whales are still commonly seen in the area, although not in the same numbers as before.

Finally, the right whale (*arvik; Balaena mysticotus*) has almost completely disappeared from Hudson Strait, hunted as it was by European and American whalers who operated from south Baffin Island at the end of the nineteenth century. The finback whale, the narwhal (*allanguaq; Monodon monoceros*), and the killer whale (*aarluk; Orcinus orca*) are relatively rare sights.[7]

The most important land mammal is the caribou (*tuttuq; Rangifer arcticus*). Once present everywhere in Nunavik, these animals disappeared from the northern tundra at the beginning of the twentieth century. Until the end of the 1970s Quaqtamiut had to travel to the wooded areas around Tasiujaq (Leaf Bay) and Kuujjuaq to hunt them. Caribou made a rapid comeback during the 1980s and are now found again in great numbers in the vicinity of Tuvaaluk.[8] Thus, the caribou has regained its importance as a staple food, though not as a material for making clothes.

The wolf (*amaruq; Canis lupus*) came back with the caribou, becoming somewhat of a nuisance. There are several recent accounts of hunters being attacked or nearly attacked by hungry wolves.

The arctic fox (*tiriganniaq; Alopex lagopus*) and the red fox (*tiriganniaq kajuq; Vulpes fulva*) are mainly found inland, although some also live on the coast and coastal islands. With a demographic cycle similar to that of their main staple, the lemming (*avinngaq*), fox become plentiful about once or twice every four years. They are not as widely trapped as they once were because their fur has now lost most of its commercial value.

Some other fur bearers that are occasionally met include the wolverine (*qavvik; Gulo luscus*), the otter (*pamiurtuuq; Lutra canadensis*), the mink (*kuutsiuti; Mustella vison*), and the arctic hare (*ukaliq; Lepus arcticus*).

On the coast, chiefly in winter, one finds the polar bear (*nanuq; Thalarctos maritimus*). Travelling on the floating ice pans, most polar bears come from Akpatok, where they summer.

The Tuvaaluk region is home to many species of birds. Some of them, such as the ptarmigan (*aqiggiq; Lagopus lagopus*), the seagull (*naujaq; Larus argentatus* and *Larus hyperboreus*), the raven (*tulugaq; Corvus corax*), the white owl (*uppialuk; Nyctea nyctea*), and the tiny snow bunting (*qupanuaq; Plectrophenax nivalis*) are year-round residents. Only ptarmigans are regularly eaten.[9] In April and May some low hills south of Tuvaaluk are literally covered with them.

The snow goose (*kanguq; Chen hyperborea*), the Canada goose (*nirliq; Branta canadensis*), and the barnacle goose (*nirlinaq; Branta bernicla*) fly through the area in May–June and September–October, during their spring and fall migrations. Some nest in the marshes of the eastern and southeastern shores of Tuvaaluk.

The eider duck (*mitiq; Somateria mollissima*) and the guillemot (*pitsiulaaq; Cephus grylle*) arrive at the same time as the geese. In June great numbers of ducks build their nests on the Tuvaaluk and Ungava coastal islands. In fall they abound on the eastern shore of Tuvaaluk, particularly when the wind blows in from the sea.

Other migratory species include the loon (*tuulliq, kallulik, qarsauq*; three species belonging to the genus *Gavia*) and the murre (*appaq; Uria lonvia*). All these birds are hunted during spring and fall. Quaqtamiut travel to the islands of the Ungava coast in June to gather eider duck eggs and eider-down.

In the lakes and streams south and southeast of Tuvaaluk, whitefish (*kavisilik; Coregonus clupeiformis*) are found, as well as grey, red, and speckled trout (*isiuralittaaq, ivitaaruq, nutilliq* respectively; they belong to the genera *Cristivomer* and *Salvelinus*). In summer arctic char (*Iqaluppik; Salvelinus alpinus* ) can be caught at the mouths of three rivers, two southwest of Tuvaaluk and one on the Ungava coast. At the end of August the char swim towards neighbouring lakes (e.g., Iqaluppilik or Ammalurtuuq), where they winter.

Finally, two edible species of fish are found in sea water, the tomcod (*uugaq; Boreogadus saida*) and the sculpin (*kanajuq; Oncocottus hexacornis*). Quaqtamiut also eat mussels (*uviluq*), clams (*ammuumajuuq*), barnacles (*ajurnaq*), and periwinkles (*kauttungajaq*). Recently scallops have begun to be harvested in Tuvaaluk.

# 1

# *Qallunaaqalaurtinagu:*
# When There Were No Qallunaat

To understand how modern Inuit came to be what they now are requires a knowledge of history. Even if their way of life is increasingly similar to that of southern Canadians, many Inuit cultural values and social habits cannot be explained without reference to aboriginal tradition. Quaqtamiut are no exception, and to them diachrony is important. In reflecting on their own past, they often establish a distinction between two periods in the development of the Tuvaaluk area and of Nunavik in general, the one before and the one after Qallunaat established themselves in the North. The first, *qallunaaqalaurtinagu* 'when there were no Qallunaat,' plays a crucial part in the definition of their identity. For this was the time of the *inutuinnait* 'the genuine Inuit,' those who knew how to survive by themselves, without the help of modern technology.

Quaqtamiut are conscious of the genealogical continuity between these *inutuinnait* and themselves, but, at the same time, they realize that their culture changed markedly after contact with Qallunaat. To shed some light on this process of continuity and change, this chapter will describe how the ancestors of today's Quaqtamiut lived in the old times and how they came into contact with Euro-Canadians. To enrich our historical knowledge, data from 'official' history, written by professional archaeologists, anthropologists, and historians, will deliberately be mixed here with information drawn from the memories of the Quaqtaq people.

## Prehistory

The ancestors of the contemporary Inuit, Yupik, and Aleut populations crossed Bering Strait, from Asia to North America,[1] between 9000 and 7000 years ago. We do not know for sure why they migrated out of their Asian homeland, but it seems probable that they were searching for new hunting grounds. Like their descendants, these people were well adapted to an arctic and subarctic environment. They hunted caribou, seal, and whale; lived in stone and sod houses or in skin tents; and practised shamanism. Their language shared several elements with modern Inuit and Yupit.

Archaeological evidence shows that about 4000 years BC, these ancestors were living in what is now central western Alaska, around Norton Sound and the Bering Sea. Between 3000 and 2000 BC, they developed a new culture whose technology was characterized by small tools and hunting implements made of stone. This culture, which may be considered to be the first truly Eskimo (Inuit and Yupik) tradition, spread over the whole North American Arctic. During the second and first millennia BC (from 4000 to 2000 years ago), Eskimo families left Alaska in increasing numbers to enter what is now Canada. Some settled in the western and central Canadian Arctic, but others reached Baffin Island, Greenland, Nunavik, Labrador, and even the island of Newfoundland.

According to archaeologists, some of these families settled in the Tuvaaluk area as early as 200 BC. The remains of their houses can still be seen on southern Qikirtaaluk Island, the southeast and southwest coasts of Tuvaaluk, and some Ungava Bay islands. Between 1975 and 1979 these remains were studied by researchers from Université du Québec à Montréal (see Plumet and Badgley 1980), who found that this first wave of settlers occupied the area from 200 BC to around AD 1530. They lived in semi-subterranean houses, and this during the various seasons of the year, and their camps generally comprised between three and five houses (Badgley 1980, Bibeau 1984). Some of these dwellings were quite large and housed several families, a fact that led some archaeologists to believe that these structures had not been built by an Eskimo population, but by Scandinavian Vikings (Lee 1979). Such longhouses can be found on southern Qikirtaaluk and at Qilalugarsiuvik, in the Ungava islands (Plumet 1985), as well as around Kangirsuk and in other areas of the Arctic.

These people, whose culture is called 'Dorset' by archaeologists, subsisted on hunting, fishing, and the gathering of various plants and of animal products. A study of the bone remains found in their Qikirtaaluk houses (Julien 1980) showed that the animals (such as seal, caribou, and walrus) hunted and eaten by these first Tuvaalummiut were quite the same as those sought by modern Quaqtaqmiut.

Around the year AD 1000, the climate began to warm up a little, and large sea mammals, most notably the whale, were now able to penetrate the northernmost waters of the Canadian and Greenlandic Arctic. This spurred a second wave of migration. Small bands of Alaskan hunters, equipped with better kayaks, sleds, and harpoons than their Dorset predecessors, followed the whales and entered Canada. The new technology they had developed, the Thule culture, gave them mobility and efficiency. This explains why it took them only a few hundred years to occupy the entire North American Arctic, from northwestern Alaska to eastern Greenland. These people, whose language had over the years become somewhat different from that of the other Eskimo populations, were the direct ancestors of present-day Inuit.

The first Thule Inuit seem to have reached the Tuvaaluk area about AD 1100, some nine hundred years ago. According to archaeologists, their main settlement was at Illutalik, on Igloo Island, in the southernmost section of the bay. They hunted whale, walrus, seal, and caribou, and they fished and gathered food. During the summer they lived in skin tents, but in early fall they built (or reoccupied) half-buried stone and sod houses in which they spent part of the winter. Most later moved into snow houses, where they remained until spring.

When the Thule people arrived, Dorset Eskimos already occupied the larger part of the area. The two groups seem to have cohabited, without much mingling,[2] for some four hundred years. They spoke different, though related, languages[3] because they shared the same Bering Sea Eskimo ancestors. Dorset preferred to settle nearer to open water (their main sites were on Qikirtaaluk and the Ungava coast islands), whereas Thule dwelt in the southernmost part of Tuvaaluk.

At the beginning of the sixteenth century, that is, between 1500 and 1530, the Dorset Eskimos finally disappeared. They probably merged with the Thule Inuit and were assimilated by them. Across the entire North American Arctic, Tuvaaluk is the place where the Dorset culture survived the longest (Plumet 1978). Its bearers are well remembered by the modern offspring of the Thule people, who call them the Tuniit, and tell many stories about their doings.

The history of Tuvaaluk thus extends over two thousand years. The area is rich in game, and for this reason it has been continuously occupied by human beings since about 200 BC. Many prehistoric archaeological sites are still visited by modern hunters and, until recently, were regularly used as winter, spring, or summer camps. Quaqtamiut are thus heirs to a very ancient cultural tradition.

## The Culture of the *Inutuinnait*

This tradition evolved over centuries, but many of its original components are still to be found in contemporary Inuit culture. For Quaqtamiut this culture is best represented by the *inutuinnait*. These are the 'genuine Inuit,' who occupied Nunavik before the advent of Qallunaat technology and institutions[4] and those among their descendants who remain able to live by themselves on the land, as their forefathers did. In the eyes of many contemporaries, the *inutuinnait* epitomize what a real Inuk should be. Until recently the word was commonly used to draw a distinction between ethnic Inuit ('the genuine human beings'), in general, and the other (non-Eskimo) human beings (such as Indians or Qallunaat; see Dorais 1988). But, nowadays, one increasingly hears from both Inuit and Qallunaat assertions to the effect that modern Inuit are not *inutuinnait* any more because they have adopted Euro-Canadian culture.

The memories of the older Quaqtamiut,[5] as well as archival and ethnographic research undertaken by anthropologists such as Turner (1979 [1894]), Saladin d'Anglure (1967, 1984), and Vézinet (1982), have enabled me to offer the following reconstruction of the way of life of the Tuvaaluk people at the turn of the twentieth century, just before the establishment of permanent Qallunaat installations in the northwestern Ungava area.

The population of the Tuvaaluk region was never very high (Vézinet 1982). Around 1870 no more than ten families lived in the area. Most of these belonged to a group of relatives headed by a man named Aqiggialuk, who had his own *umiaq* 'large skin boat.' Some thirty years later (1895–1905) the leading families, each of whom also had an *umiaq*, were those of two brothers, Inuguluaraq and Aanaqattaq. These were very mobile people. They seem to have spent some years in the Tuvaaluk area, before leaving for other regions and, eventually, coming back to Tuvaaluk. In the 1910s and 1920s there were no more than twenty to thirty permanent Tuvaalummiut,[6] but some additional families[7] visited the region from time to time. Most of these people now have grandchildren and great-grandchildren living in Quaqtaq, Kangirsuk, or Kangiqsujuaq.

At the end of the nineteenth century Tuvaalummiut occupied small seasonal hunting camps (*nunaliit*) of no more than five or six households each. On average, for example, five families were to be found at Iggiajaq (see Map 2) in wintertime, two at Imilik (in spring), two at Quaqtaq in fall. Despite abundant natural resources, the advancement of technology was not sufficient for a higher density of population.

Quaqtaq did not yet exist as a village.[8] It was a seasonal hunting camp, occupied principally during fall. No structure built of hard materials was to be found in the Tuvaaluk area. The people spent their winters in snow houses (*illu* or *illuvigaq*) and their summers in skin tents (*tupiq*).

All the families migrated periodically from one camp to another. This way of life enabled them to exploit the natural resources available in each season. Over a typical year people occupied three or four different camps. All of these were situated within the Tuvaaluk region, but interregional mobility was quite high, with several families spending some years in neighbouring areas such as Kangirsuk or Kangiqsujuaq before eventually returning to Tuvaaluk. It also happened that families from these neighbouring regions spent more or less extended periods (from a season to several years) in the Tuvaaluk area, generally sharing campsites with the Tuvaalummiut. Far from being closed units, the Inuit hunting territories were thus open to everybody, provided the new arrivals behaved correctly and cooperated with the local population.

People sharing a camp were generally close relatives, most often a group of married siblings living with their parents, if these were still alive. Brothers tended to remain together, their sisters often going to live with their husbands' relatives. However, a newlywed son-in-law might live with his wife's parents, for a year or so, before moving with his own relatives. Despite this patrilocal bias, Inuit kinship was – and still is – bilateral. Nothing forced brothers to stick together, or their sisters to move elsewhere. People tried to find the best residential arrangements. Frequently this involved the coresidence and collaboration of a group of male hunters knowing and trusting each other. Because brothers with their father precisely answered this definition, male siblings often preferred to live and hunt together. Nevertheless, even when immediate relatives shared the same camping location, each nuclear family, which included at least two children, had its own tent or snow house. Sometimes these individual igloos opened onto a common entranceway, a construction pattern that enabled people to visit each other without having to go outside.

A semi-nomadic residential grouping whose members are relatives is called a local band (Helm 1965). Most Tuvaaluk camps used to form local bands. As we shall see in the following chapters, this pattern of organization, where residence and social solidarities are based on kinship relations, still survives in the North, and it constitutes an important factor for understanding present-day community life.

At the winter camp the men harpooned seal at the animals' breathing holes, while the women (and, sometimes, men too) fished in the neighbouring lakes. Some people trapped fox around the camp. At the beginning of the twentieth century, however, this activity had not yet gained the importance it would attain a few years later, after fox skins had become a commercial commodity, and men started to undertake long trapping journeys inland from Tuvaaluk.

Each year, at the end of May families would move to their spring camps (e.g., Airartuuq, Salliq, Imilik, or Illutalik), where men hunted seal basking on the ice (*uuttuq*) or harpooned seal and beluga from the shore (*utaqqiuvik*). As soon as the sea ice began to break away from the land, the hunters went after these animals in their kayaks (*qajaq*), continuing to do so all summer long. In addition to their regular domestic duties, including cooking, flensing skins, and mending clothes, women gathered eggs and eiderdown from the nesting sites on the Ungava coast and islands.

In August most families would hunt caribou around Tuvaaluk. They built, or used already built, rows of stone cairns (*inutsuit*) that looked more or less like human beings. Women and children tried to scare the animals, in order to drive them towards the men who hid behind the cairns, shooting at the caribou with their bows and arrows when the herd passed by. In September some families would join with the Kangirsuk people who went caribou hunting inland (near Tasirjuaq, Payne Lake), by way of the Payne River (Kangirsuup kuunga). Women and children travelled in large open skin boats (*umiaq*), while the men paddled their kayaks. A few individuals remained inland all winter long, subsisting on fish and caribou meat (Vézinet 1980), but most families came back to the coast in October.

The men who had remained on the seashore hunted sea mammals from their kayaks till freeze-up time. Those owning an *umiaq* would use it to move between campsites and to hunt beluga and walrus. In late summer women went berry picking. Before winter started they had to sew new sets of caribou-skin clothes for their family. During summer and early fall, men and women fished arctic char at the mouths of the region's few rivers, using lines or stone weirs (*saputiit*). In fall and spring there also was much bird hunting.

When the newly fallen snow was deep enough, people returned to their winter camp (mostly to Iggiajaq or Iqaluppilik), where snow houses were built. Wintertime activities resumed, including travel by sled and dog team. Since the 1870s some individuals had been visiting Fort Chimo (Kuujjuaq) Hudson's Bay Company (HBC) trading post once a year, usually leaving Tuvaaluk in March.

Most of the time those who worked together at catching game belonged to the same extended family or local band. The men hunted, fished, made tools and hunting gear, built the snow house, paddled their kayaks or drove their dog teams, while the women cooked, flensed the skins, sewed and mended the clothes, skin boats, and tents, tended the lamp,[9] fished, gathered seasonal products, trapped, helped with caribou hunting, and rowed the *umiaq*. Children learned by imitating their parents' activities and were entrusted with responsibilities adapted to their gender and age.

All game collectively caught was divided among those who had taken part in its capture, each hunter receiving a share corresponding to his participation. At the community level, surplus game was distributed among all those in need of food and skins. The first game of each species caught by a boy was given to the midwife (*arnaquti*) who had helped his mother deliver him, and this person shared the game with the whole camp. Similarly, a girl offered to her mother's midwife (*sanaji*) the first clothes she had sewn by herself.

Before their conversion to Christianity the *inutuinnait* practised shamanism. They believed the world to be peopled by numerous spirits, some good, some bad, and some indifferent. One bad spirit, Amautilialuk ('the one with a baby-carrying pouch'), an ogre, lived at Illutalialuk, south of Tuvaaluk. He killed with an axe those who approached his house, carrying them away in his pouch (*amauti*) to eat them. Another spirit (a *tuurngaq*, a shaman's helper) lived in a cavern near Airartuuq, on the Ungava coast. Goblins (*inugagulligait*) were also known to dwell at Qikirtaujaq (on the seashore, halfway between Tuvaaluk and Kangirsuk). Despite their small size, their strength was herculean. They were able to carry half a walrus on their shoulders.

Human beings had three souls. One, *anirniq* 'the breath,' disappeared at death; the second, *tarniq* 'the shadow,' survived the body and went to live in the sky or underground; the third one, *atiq* 'the name,' was transmitted to newborn babies and continued its existence inside a new body. As we shall see in Chapter 4, these beliefs about the soul are still alive today in Quaqtaq.

The shaman (*angakkuq*), whether a man or a woman, knew how to contact spirits and benefit from their help. He or she was thus able to heal the sick, improve the weather, or bring game back. In the wintertime shamans often held public performances in the *qaggiq*, a large ceremonial snow house with enough room for the entire population of a camp.

Each camp had its own shaman. We do not know for sure who the Tuvaaluk *angakkuit* were, but people remember the last four shamans from the neighbouring Kangiqsujuaq area (Saladin d'Anglure 1967, 1984): Pilurtuut, who served as a shaman till the end of the 1920s, is said to have been repeatedly run through with a harpoon, without suffering any wound. Qasinga, a woman, had a river as her spirit helper, and water flowed out of her mouth when she spoke. The other two shamans were Alariaq and Auvvik.

The *inutuinnait* had their own rules of good behaviour (see Qumaq 1988 for a description of some of them). When somebody departed from these rules, he or she was ostracized, that is, nobody spoke or interacted with him or her, as long as he or she did not behave correctly. A criminal offender (say, a murderer or a very violent individual) was sometimes killed by his victim's son or brother or by a man designated for this task by the other men of the camp. During summer, when two or several local bands met at the caribou hunting grounds or elsewhere, the bands' leaders (often the eldest males and/or best hunters) challenged each other to a singing competition, with the winner being the one who ridiculed his opponent the most. These competitions released tensions that may have otherwise led to fights. One great singer was Angutinnguaq, from the Kangiqsujuaq and Salluit areas, who also spent some seasons around Tuvaaluk.

## Early Contacts with the Qallunaat

In 1773 the Moravian missionary Jens Haven[10] drew up a list of the main Inuit settlements northwest of Nain, Labrador. Among the ten or so place-names found on this list, one, which Haven calls *Tuak*, probably corresponds to Tuvaaluk. This would thus be the very first mention of the Tuvaaluk area in the written literature. On the basis of Haven's data, ethnohistorian Garth Taylor (1975) estimated at about a hundred persons the population of the Tuvaalummiut in 1773; this figure positions the region among the most densely populated areas of Nunavik at the end of the eighteenth century.

In 1811 two other Moravian missionaries, brothers Kohlmeister and Kmoch, reached Kuujjuaq. They heard about an important settlement named *Tuvaq*, at the northwestern corner of Ungava Bay (Vézinet 1982). Here, again, Tuvaaluk appears to have been one of the principal dwelling areas of Nunavik.

After that, however, no reference to the place is to be found in the literature, even if throughout the nineteenth century, a growing number of Qallunaat explorers, scientists, traders, and missionaries visited the Ungava Bay area. The otherwise excellent ethnographic descriptions by Turner (1894), Payne (1899), and Hawkes (1916) do not even mention the Tuvaalummiut. Low (1906) is the only one to note that, in 1893, 115 Inuit were living on Hudson Strait, between Cape Hopes Advance (Nuvuk) and Cape Weggs (northwest of Kangiqsujuaq). It seems probable that no more than fifty of these people dwelt around Tuvaaluk at this time, a decrease in the population since the late eighteenth century, which might be explained by the quasi-complete disappearance of the whale from the Hudson Strait and Ungava Bay waters.

In 1830 the Hudson's Bay Company established a trading post at Fort Chimo (Kuujjuaq). The post closed down in 1842, but reopened for good in 1866. From the 1870s on the Tuvaalummiut, like other northern Nunavik Inuit (*Tarramiut* 'people of the North'), began sending some individuals to trade at Fort Chimo once a year, during winter.

In 1899 Anglican missionaries opened a base near the HBC store. The annual trading expeditions thus provided the Inuit opportunities to hear about Christianity and learn the syllabic writing system that missionaries had introduced. As a consequence, Tarramiut converted, and by the end of the 1920s almost all of them had become Christian and literate in their language.

The establishment of the HBC trading post fostered important changes in the technology and economic activities of Tuvaalummiut. Since at least the seventeenth century the Nunavik people had known the use of metal (*kikiak*), obtained – mostly in the form of iron nails and knife blades – through trade with the Labrador Inuit and, perhaps, the Montagnais, Naskapi, and Cree Indians.[11] They later also obtained a few guns.

But until the last quarter of the nineteenth century the traditional raw materials – stone, bone, and ivory – were still widely in use, especially among Tarramiut, for manufacturing knives, blades (for harpoons, spears, and arrows), and sewing needles. By 1880, however, the Hudson Strait people, including the Tuvaalummiut, already were in possession of a relatively high number of guns, fish nets, and metal traps, obtained from the HBC at Fort Chimo.[12] They were also familiar with tobacco, flour, tea, and sugar (Graburn 1969).

By the beginning of the twentieth century metal had definitively replaced the older materials, and between 1910 and 1914 the use of guns and steel traps became universal in Tuvaaluk and other Tarramiut areas. According to Vézinet (1982), some traditional hunting implements (e.g., the bow, arrow, and caribou spear) remained in limited use. Until recently, the small harpoon (*unaaq*) was still used for retrieving seals killed with a gun from a boat.

The introduction of the steel trap greatly increased the efficacy of the trappers. One of the reasons why the HBC had established itself in Nunavik was that it was interested in buying the fur of the arctic fox. The traders thus encouraged the Inuit men to undertake long (two to three weeks) trapping expeditions inland, during winter, and to sell their catch to the store. The pattern of economic activities changed, as most Inuit families, instead of hunting exclusively for themselves and their relatives, became increasingly dependent on food, cloth, and other goods obtained at the trading post in exchange for their fox fur and sealskins. Because the skins of seal (and, to a lesser extent, caribou) had become commercial commodities, they were replaced, in their domestic uses, by store-bought equivalents. As a consequence, by 1920 most Tuvaalummiut wore clothes made of textiles, and the canvas tent and Peterhead boat (a craft, nine to ten metres long, propelled by a sail and/or inboard engine) had completely replaced the traditional skin *tupiq* and *umiaq*.

After 1900 trapping had become so lucrative that the HBC and other traders (e.g., the French company Révillon Frères) decided to establish trading posts nearer to the Inuit camps. In 1909 the HBC opened a store at Cape Wolstenholme, near present-day Ivujivik, at the western entrance to Hudson Strait. Nearer to Tuvaaluk, Révillon established a post at Kangiqsujuaq in 1910, and the HBC did likewise in 1914. In 1921 both companies opened stores in Kangirsuk. The stage was thus set for the complete inclusion of Tuvaalummiut into the modern world.

# 2

# The Formation of a Community

The culture and history of the *inutuinnait* form the basis on which the identity and community organization of Quaqtaq were built. However, only with the establishment of Euro-Canadian trading posts, and other institutions in the area, did the economic and social conditions leading to the emergence of Tuvaaluk as a centre of permanent settlement progressively get put into place.

If a date is to be chosen to mark the start of Quaqtaq's modern history, it should be 1927. That year an independent trader by the name of Herbert Hall, whom the Inuit remember as Isumataaluk ('the big chief'), established a small store at Iggiajaq, in southern Tuvaaluk (see Appendix A). The following year (1928) the federal Department of Transport opened a weather station at Nuvuk (Cape Hopes Advance), to provide southern Canada – by wireless telegraphy – information on temperature, snow, and ice conditions.[1]

The store and the weather station were the first Qallunaat establishments in the Tuvaaluk area. Their presence encouraged Inuit settlement, and in 1931 the federal census (quoted in Vézinet 1982) listed a total of 105 Tuvaalummiut, which was an unprecedented number since, probably, the first third of the nineteenth century. In 1932 a second store was opened at Iggiajaq, this time by Jean Berthé (Ijautialuuk, 'the big spectacles'), who worked for the French traders Révillon Frères.

The benefits brought by the stores were evident; Tuvaalummiut were provided with traps, guns, ammunition, and basic goods (such as cloth, flour, tea, sugar, and tobacco) in exchange for their furs. The weather station was also the source of several benefits; it employed a local family for janitorial duties, hired all available men when the annual supply ship had to be unloaded, and served as an unofficial distributor of items such as food, oil, and gasoline in consideration of various types of services rendered by the Inuit.

In this period Quaqtaq received its current name and, because of its proximity to the floe edge and to the Nuvuk weather station, became a major dwelling place. Up to then the site had been called Nuvukutaaq ('the long point'). But, as told by the late Jiimi Kuuttuq (Koneak), one day, some time in the early 1930s, Isumataaluk (Herbert Hall), who hunted beluga at Nuvukutaaq, was obliged to heed the call of nature. Because his faeces were alive with parasites, his Inuit companions called the place Quaqtaq, 'the intestinal worm,' the name that rapidly went into general use.[2]

In this chapter, I will show how Quaqtaq developed from a winter camp in the 1940s and 1950s and a sedentary village in the 1960s to a full-fledged municipality in the early 1980s.

## The Tuvaaluk Camps

In 1936, throughout the Arctic, the Révillon Frères trading posts either closed down or began operating as Hudson's Bay Company stores, after the French company was bought out by its rival. Révillon's Iggiajaq establishment then became an outpost of the HBC store at Kangirsuk, and Berthé left for Kangiqsujuaq, where he opened an independent trading operation.

Two years later, in the summer 1938, five families, all of whom had been Berthé's regular customers, decided to follow him back to Tuvaaluk, where hunting and trapping conditions appeared promising. These were the families of Inuluk, Nua Masik, Nuvvukat, Miqquluk, and Tirtiluk. They travelled in two boats, one belonging to Inuluk and Nua, the other to Nuvvukat, Miqquluk, and Tirtiluk. After a few months Berthé and the Tirtiluk family left for Kangirsuk, but the others remained in the area. One of the newcomers, Inuluk, took charge of the HBC store.

This migration is still vividly remembered by several elders, who either took part in it as youngsters or witnessed the boats' arrival in Tuvaaluk. About half of present-day Quaqtamiut are descended from these migrants, who may thus be considered as belonging to the founders of the community.

In 1938, too, Isumataaluk, who was still operating his Iggiajaq trading post, fell gravely ill. In early winter he had to leave by dogsled for Kuujjuaq, where he hoped to find medical aid. Unfortunately, for him, his illness was too far advanced, and he died before he got there. In 1939 Hall's store was bought out by the Baffin Trading Company (BTC). This was a small commercial firm headed by a trader named James Cantley, who spent a few weeks at Iggiajaq, before entrusting a local hunter, Taqulik, with management of the post.

The start of the Second World War, in 1939–40, dealt a severe blow to the fur trade. Many smaller stores had to cease operations. Among them, the HBC outpost at Iggiajaq closed its doors in 1940. However, this did not prevent people from continuing to settle in the Tuvaaluk area.[3] In 1940 and 1941 two brothers, Taqqiapik and Jaiku, moved to Iggiajaq[4] with their families, attracted there, they said, by two factors: plentiful game and the presence of the BTC store. They also should be counted among the founders of the modern community.

After the death of Isumataaluk some families left Iggiajaq for Quaqtaq, which was nearer the limit of land-fast ice, where sea mammals were abundant in winter. A few people moved as early as 1939–40. They were soon followed by others, for example, the family of Inuluk (in fall 1941) and those of Taqqiapik and Jaiku (in spring 1942). Quaqtaq thus developed into a major winter camp, destined to become the principal dwelling place of Tuvaalummiut.

Inuluk's move to Quaqtaq seems to have been motivated by the fact that he did not get along very well with his brother, Nua Masik. Masik remained in Iggiajaq, while Inuluk, his family, and his friend, Taqqiapik (whose children would later marry those of Inuluk), went to Quaqtaq. As shall be seen in Chapter 4, this split between the two brothers still survives in Quaqtaq's present-day kin groups.

*Tuvaaluk in 1942–3*

In 1942–3 the only permanent dwellings in the Tuvaaluk area were the three or four wooden buildings of the Nuvuk weather station, which, because of the war, operated in the summertime only, and a few cabins at Iggiajaq, which had been used as stores, warehouses, and residences by the various traders who had lived there.[5] Only one trading post (at Iggiajaq), belonging to the BTC but managed by a local Inuk, was still in operation in 1942–3, mainly during winter.

The seventy-eight residents of Tuvaaluk[6] lived in canvas tents or snow houses, according to the season. In late May 1942 fifteen families (see Table 1) moved from their winter camps to Inutsulik and, a month later, to Airartuuq, on the Ungava coast. They spent spring and summer there, the men hunting seal from the shore (*utaqqiuvik*) and, later on (in July) from their kayaks and Peterheads, while the women devoted themselves to various

TABLE 1

Distribution of the Population in the Main Tuvaaluk Camps, 1942–3

*Airartuuq, 1 August 1942 (husband/wife)*

| | |
|---|---|
| Jupi Paaliaq/Matiilita | Saami Nasaq/Ruuta |
| Sakkariasi/Taalasi | Samuili/Mini |
| Saali Quiliq/Saaliti | Qungiaq/Maqu |
| Taqqiapik/Taqaq | Inuluk/Arjangajuk (Ittukuluapik) |
| Jaiku/Lali | Miqquluk (single) |
| Alik/Inuppak | Nua Masik/Iiva |
| Matiusi Kululaaq/Aani Anautaq | Uqittuq/Tajara |
| Nuvvukat/Mini | |

*Iggiajaq, 1 January 1943 (husband/wife)*

| | |
|---|---|
| Samuili/Mini | Nuvvukat/Mini |
| Miqquluk (single) | Nua Masik/Iiva |
| Matiusi Kululaaq/Aani Anautaq | Tajara (widow) |
| Inugaluaq (widow) | Taqulik/Miaji Masik |
| Maakusi Kiliutaq/Luusi | Nunalik/Niqiguluk |

*Quaqtaq, 1 January 1943 (husband/wife)*

| | |
|---|---|
| Qungiaq/Maqu | Inuluk/Arjangajuk (Ittukuluapik) |
| Saali Quiliq/Saaliti | Taqqiapik/Taqaq |
| Jaiku/Lali | Alik/Inuppak |
| Kuuttuq/Maata | |

domestic tasks (including the preparation of skins for trading). During summer the hunters also went after walrus and beluga, and they organized fishing expeditions to the lakes south of Tuvaaluk.

In late August 1942 the six families who had spent the previous winter in Iggiajaq returned there from Airartuuq. At the end of October they were joined by four other families, who had summered on various islands within Tuvaaluk. In the meantime, those who had lived in Quaqtaq the preceding winter returned there, while two more households moved to Iqaluppilik, on the Ungava coast.

In the fall and winter of 1942–3, then, a total of ten families lived in Iggiajaq, seven in Quaqtaq, and two at Iqaluppilik (Table 1). Some of these families were close relatives. In Quaqtaq, for example, five out of seven households were related in various ways. Residence, though, was not exclusively motivated by kinship. Some brothers and sisters found it more profitable to live in different camps during winter because this enabled them to gain access to a wider basin of natural resources. Thus, there were several cases of sibling groups spread out between Iggiajaq and Quaqtaq.

The men continued to hunt seal from their kayaks during fall. They generally left together in the morning, often before daybreak. As soon as the snow cover was sufficient to enable travel by sled and dog team, the hunters started trapping fox. This activity, which had developed tremendously over the preceding decades, was very important to the Iggiajaq people, whose geographical location, in the southernmost part of Tuvaaluk, gave them easy access to the inland trapping territories. Quaqtamiut were also trappers, but the proximity of the floe edge incited them to devote a lot of time to seal hunting.

Each individual trapper or pair of trappers possessed his or their own trapline, that is, a fixed itinerary along which the traps were disposed. Some set up their trapline by themselves, but others had been taught the itinerary by somebody else, usually their father or an elder brother. Trapping was the main source of cash, the principal *raison d'être* of the trading posts being to buy fox (and, to a lesser extent, seal) skins from the Inuit. Some trappers left for several weeks at a time, and often they brought back dozens of skins. When fox were plentiful, seal hunting was completely set aside.

The camps were small collaborative units, whose members hunted together and shared the food they caught. There were no chiefs, but the heads of extended families, as well as the best hunters and trappers, held a real measure of authority. Since at least the 1920s all Tuvaalummiut had become Anglican Christians, and the principal camps (i.e., Iggiajaq, Quaqtaq, and Airartuuq) had one or two lay readers (*tutsiatitsiji* 'the one who makes people pray'), often elders or family heads, who presided over the Sunday service and acted in various ways as moral counsellors. It is noteworthy that, in 1942–3, the two Inuit outpost managers, Inuluk and Taqulik, also played the part of lay readers. They thus held economic, social (as family heads), and spiritual power.

*Tuvaaluk in 1956*

As years passed by camp life remained essentially unchanged, although a few important events modified the distribution of the population within

Tuvaaluk. At the end of the war, in 1945, the weather station resumed its winter operations, and the Baffin Trading Company post received a Qallunaaq manager. The BTC had problems, however, competing with the much stronger HBC. The Iggiajaq post kept a very limited supply of goods, and when these were exhausted, Tuvaalummiut had to travel to Kangirsuk to trade at the HBC establishment. As a consequence, the Iggiajaq store closed for good in 1949.

In the meantime, a Róman Catholic mission had been established in Quaqtaq in 1947. Its founder, Umikallak, 'the short beard' (Father André Steinmann, OMI) had chosen to settle there, rather than in Iggiajaq, because, in his opinion, Quaqtaq had three main advantages: it was a major camp, easily accessible by sea, and free from outside influences (no other Qallunaat dwelt there).

Umikallak reached Quaqtaq by boat, from Kangiqsujuaq,[7] in August 1947 (Steinmann 1977). First, he built a chapel–residence, then a tiny store where tobacco, matches, soap, and a very limited supply of various domestic products were available for sale. The missionary also acted as a first aid nurse. The following year he began to teach class to the children, and to a few women, wintering in Quaqtaq. They were taught the syllabic writing characters,[8] basic mathematics, and some rudiments of English. Despite these efforts, however, Umikallak and his successors were only able to convert a small handful of Tuvaalummiut. There were never more than fifteen to twenty Catholics living in the area at the same time. In the twenty years of its existence, though, the mission played an important part as provider of services and community centre, where people gathered at Christmas and Eastertime and on various other occasions.

After the Second World War the federal government felt an obligation to offer to its northern residents most of the services available to southern Canadians. It thus began to intervene more directly in the welfare and administration of the Inuit. In 1947–8 Ottawa started distributing family allowances to all families with children. In eastern Nunavik the distribution process was entrusted to Royal Canadian Mounted Police (RCMP) officers stationed at Kuujjuaq. The allowances took the form of vouchers exchangeable for basic goods, at the Kangirsuk HBC store.

From 1950 a federal patrol ship, the *C.D. Howe* (Mattavik 'the place to undress'), started calling once a year at Quaqtaq, as well as at most other eastern Arctic communities. Its medical team examined the population, assessing its health problems, mending teeth, and treating hearing and sight defects. Those diagnosed with tuberculosis or other severe illnesses were immediately put aboard the ship, to be sent to a southern hospital on returning to Montreal at the end of the summer. In spite of basic medical care, however, an epidemic of measles (*aupartukallait* 'the small red things') swept over the Ungava area in March–April 1952. In these two months eleven adults, more than 10 per cent of the total population, died in Tuvaaluk (see Appendix B).

After 1943 Quaqtaq continued to grow at the expense of Iggiajaq. The establishment of the mission (1947) and the closing of the BTC store (in 1949) tolled the knell of the latter camp. In fall 1950 the last families to have spent the preceding winter in Iggiajaq decided to move to Quaqtaq.

Between 1944 and 1953 six families migrated to Tuvaaluk, four of them from the Kangiqsujuaq area and two from Kangirsuk. Only three households moved out of the region during this same period, two of them coming back after a few years. All these people settled in Quaqtaq, rather than Iggiajaq. Their motivations for moving to Tuvaaluk were linked to family matters. Five out of six immigrant households had close relatives already living in the area. The exception was a Roman Catholic family who accompanied Umikallak in 1947 to help him with the mission.

On 1 January 1956[9] Tuvaaluk had a population of 108 Inuit (twenty-five families), plus four Qallunaat (the missionary and the three employees of the weather station). Seven Tuvaalummiut temporarily resided outside Nunavik during 1956, spending more or less extended periods in southern hospitals. The composition of the population had changed quite a lot since the early 1940s. More than half (eleven of twenty) of the hunters active in 1942 were now deceased (see Appendix B), and several new families had immigrated from outside. All departed family heads, though, left married children in the Tuvaaluk area, thus ensuring a remarkable genealogical continuity.

In 1956 twenty of the twenty-five families shared the same migratory pattern. They lived more than nine months of the year in Quaqtaq or its immediate vicinity (see Table 2), spending the balance of their time in Inutsulik and Airartuuq. The other five households occupied various outlying camps.

In spite of its demographic importance, Quaqtaq was not a real village yet. Except for the mission, there were no permanent buildings on the site. The resident families still lived in snow houses or tents, depending on the season. Three households, however, occupied two small wooden cabins about halfway between Quaqtaq and Nuvuk,[10] and a fourth one – who moved to Kangirsuk in March 1956 – resided at Nuvuk, where the man and his wife worked for the weather station. Between 2 and 13 June, all Quaqtamiut, including those living near Nuvuk, moved to Inutsulik,

TABLE 2

Distribution of the Population in the Tuvaaluk Camps, 15 March 1956

*Quaqtaq and vicinity (husband/wife)*

| | |
|---|---|
| Aqiggiq/Juana | Maasiu/Inuppak |
| Kuuttuq/Siaja | Jupi/Iiva |
| Samuili (widower) | Jaiku/Lali |
| Uppik/Qupirruk | Itittuuq/Qulliq |
| Matiusi/Aani Anautaq | Tuniq/Matiilita |
| Putulik/Luisa | Qamuraaluk/Qasiilinaq |
| Qarisaq/Tirisi | Miinnguq/Arpik |
| Aalupa/Suusi | Jugini (widower) |
| Ituaq/Sikuliaq | Qattaq (widow) |
| Saali/Miaji | Jimi Papikattuq/Lali |

*Iqaluppilik-on-the-lake (husband/wife)*

| | |
|---|---|
| Sirli/Siaja | Taqulik/Masik |
| Jaani/Ripika | Aqiggialuk (bachelor) |

and from there, on 2 July, to Airartuuq. They stayed on the island till 22 August when they came back to Quaqtaq for the rest of the year.

Their hunting, fishing, and trapping activities had not changed much since 1942–3. They still used dog teams, kayaks, and Peterhead boats. These large inboard motor craft, although very expensive to buy, had become a necessity for travelling to Kangirsuk, now the only trading post in the vicinity of Tuvaaluk. Their crews were fairly stable units, generally comprising close relatives who pursued many economic – and other – activities together.[11]

Apart from trading, opportunities for earning money were few and far apart, although in the 1950s they were somewhat more numerous than in the preceding decade. The mission and weather station occasionally hired people for odd jobs, and the government tried to provide the Inuit with temporary labour. In 1956, for example, most Quaqtaq men worked a few weeks for mining prospectors in the Kangirsuk area.

Five families followed a migratory pattern different from that of the majority of the population. Three of them spent the winter at Iqaluppilik (south of Tuvaaluk, near the Ungava coast), on the lakeshore, to fish char through the ice. At the end of May they moved to Salliq, about twenty kilometres to the northeast, where they remained until August, hunting seal and beluga. They then went to the Iqaluppilik seashore, where they could hunt and fish at the same time. In late October they returned to their lakeshore winter camp.

One other family spent most of the 1955–6 winter season in Iqaluppilik. In April however, they left for Ipiutaq, a campsite near Iggiajaq, where they were joined by close relatives who had wintered in the Kangirsuk area. At the end of July all these people started travelling by boat across the Tuvaaluk and Kangirsuk areas, stopping wherever game was plentiful. At the end of September they returned to Iggiajaq and Ipiutaq, where the boats were brought ashore, and in early November they moved back to winter camp.

These five marginal families were the last true nomadic Tuvaalummiut.[12] In 1956 they still maintained a pattern of migration that had not changed much since the early 1940s. The majority of the population, however, had already become almost sedentary. Even if they continued to live in tents and snow houses, people spent most of the year in one location, Quaqtaq, near the two local Qallunaat establishments: the mission, with its embryonic store and school, and the weather station. The transition from seasonal camps to permanent settlement, which led to residential modernity, was thus well on its way in the Tuvaaluk area.

**Koartak, Koartac, or Quaqtaq?**

*Sedentarization*

This transition to permanent settlement was completed by the turn of the decade. In 1957 most Quaqtamiut built themselves year-round homes. These were small (one or two rooms), stove-heated, scrapwood cabins, without water, electricity, or proper insulation. Despite their shortcomings, these buildings quickly replaced the snow houses. In the winter of 1958–9, one last family was still living in an igloo, but by the following fall they had moved into a cabin. After that, snow houses were used only as temporary dwellings, during winter travel.

In Quaqtaq the replacement of igloos by more permanent structures occurred earlier than it did elsewhere in Nunavik. This was because leftover wood, salvaged from the mission, the weather station, and the trading post site at Iggiajaq, was relatively abundant. In these cabins makeshift stoves burned brushwood and seal or beluga blubber, as well as pieces of coal (obtained from the mission) and odd scraps of wood. Meals were generally cooked on naphtha (primus) stoves.

In October or November 1958 the Iqaluppilik people decided to spend the cold season in Quaqtaq. This left only two marginal households, those of Taqulik and Maakusi Kiliutaq, who continued to winter in Iggiajaq, apart from the other Tuvaalummiut. In May 1961, however, Taqulik and his eldest son died, and his widow and his brother, Maakusi, moved to Quaqtaq with their families. Sedentarization was by then complete. Some Quaqtamiut kept the habit of spending a few weeks or a couple of months at a spring hunting camp, but from 1960 on only a minority of households went camping to Airartuuq or Salliq.

What was happening in Quaqtaq also occurred elsewhere. The period from 1955 to 1965 witnessed tremendous changes. All over the eastern Arctic the federal government was in the process of implanting a comprehensive system of social and educational services. The goal of the administration was to modernize the North, in order to make mainstream Canadians out of the Inuit. This modernization involved sedentarization, formal education, economic development, and the provision of health services.

In the late 1950s the Department of Northern Affairs (DNA) posted administrators (called Northern Service Officers[13] or NSOs) and nurses in the larger settlements (e.g., Kuujjuaq), and elementary schools began to be built in various locations. At first, Quaqtaq was deemed too small to be worth developing. The Kuujjuaq NSO even planned to transfer the whole Tuvaaluk population to Kangirsuk.[14] But when it was realized that the local people were strongly opposed to such a move, the federal bureaucrats changed their minds. In July 1960 a school was built in Quaqtaq (it burned down in early 1964, but was rebuilt the following year), along with a residence for the teacher, one for the janitor, a warehouse, and a power plant.[15]

The federal teacher, a young Anglo-Canadian bachelor, began teaching class the following September, thus bringing the academic activities of the mission to a close. The curriculum imposed by the DNA more or less copied the Ontario elementary school program, and it did not allow any place to local language and culture. Schools were meant to make 'modern Canadians' out of the Inuit, and Inuktitut was viewed as a hindrance to progress.

In addition to education, the federal government developed health and social services. The teacher was charged with distributing relief to families who could not support themselves through hunting and trapping, and, later on, he also became responsible for distributing fuel oil to those households needing it. In September 1963 the federal government built a nursing station that was to be used as living quarters when the Kuujjuaq nurse visited

Quaqtaq, two or three times a year, and which could also serve in case of epidemics. Patients suffering from tuberculosis or other severe illnesses continued to be sent to southern hospitals (by airplane rather than by boat), and until the end of the decade the *C.D. Howe* carried on with its yearly visits to Tuvaaluk.

The improvement of medical services was part of a general effort aimed at providing the Inuit with more decent living conditions. In this context, ten prefabricated wooden one-room ('matchbox') houses were brought to Quaqtaq in the summer of 1964. Four were lent to families whose heads were too old to support their relatives, and the remainder were sold on credit to other families.

Federal involvement in sectors (i.e., education and social services) that normally fall under provincial jurisdiction was justified by the fact that, in 1939, the Supreme Court of Canada had ruled that 'Eskimos are Indians' [*sic*] and, as such, dependent on Ottawa for the provision of services. At first the Quebec government was content with this arrangement and refused to have anything to do with the Nunavik Inuit. But, in June 1960, when the provincial Liberals were elected on a platform of increased economic and social autonomy for Quebec, they declared that complete governmental control over the province's natural resources was to be the main tool for achieving their goal.

Nunavik was particularly rich in minerals and had several rivers that could be harnessed for hydroelectric development. The new Quebec government considered it a strategic area and decided to participate directly in its administration (Dorais 1979). Shortly after the election, the Quebec Provincial Police (QPP) replaced the RCMP in Kuujjuaq and Great Whale River (Kuujjuaraapik), and in 1961 the government established the Direction générale du Nouveau-Québec (DGNQ), under then Minister of Natural Resources René Lévesque. As a consequence, competition developed between the federal (*kavamatuqaq* 'the old government') and provincial (*uiguikkut* 'the group of the *oui-oui* [French]') administrations.

DGNQ sent administrators to Nunavik's largest communities and, generally speaking, tried to provide the Inuit with services as yet unavailable from the federal authorities. These included radiotelephone and a post office in each village and, more importantly, Inuktitut-speaking kindergartens, the establishment of a hospital in Kuujjuaq (opened in 1967) and of a trade school in Kuujjuaraapik, and development projects specially geared to smaller settlements. In most communities the kindergartens rapidly grew into full-fledged primary schools, where Inuktitut was taught in the first grades and French in the higher classes. These offered some competition to the federal schools, which kept on teaching in English, but did not eliminate them. The provincial establishments never attracted more than 20 to 30 per cent of the school-aged children.

The provincial administration arrived in Quaqtaq in the summer of 1966, when a store and a combined kindergarten–office–residence (with a radio-telephone linking the village to the outside world) were built. The DGNQ-operated store opened on 17 October, but the kindergarten had to wait until September 1967.

Tuvaaluk was one of the last Nunavik areas to benefit from these governmental (federal and provincial) initiatives. This explains why thirteen families left the region between 1956 and 1966 to avail themselves of facilities (e.g., store, nursing station, opportunities for wage work, and better housing) still lacking in Quaqtaq. Seven of these families moved to the neighbouring communities of Kangirsuk and Kangiqsujuaq, where they already had relatives, and from which some of them had migrated to Tuvaaluk in the preceding decades. Three others left for Ivujivik and Kuujjuaq.

In 1962, at the invitation of the federal government, two of the households which had wintered at Iqaluppilik until 1958, along with a third one (consisting of three unmarried siblings), moved to Killiniq (Port Burwell), at the eastern entrance to Ungava Bay, to work for the newly established hunting and fishing cooperative. This emigration was not counterbalanced by any new arrivals. The population thus decreased a lot, reaching a low of seventy-two Quaqtamiut (thirteen families) at the end of summer 1966.

*Quaqtaq in 1966–7*

In late 1966 and early 1967 Quaqtaq was a very small community.[16] In addition to its seventy-two Inuit residents, it included a transient population of seven persons: the federal teacher, the Roman Catholic missionary, the Quebec agent (who also operated the store), the agent's wife, their baby son, and the two radio operators at the Nuvuk weather station.

Nevertheless, the village had most of the trappings of a settled establishment, including an elementary school, a store, an unmanned nursing station, and two churches (the Roman Catholic mission and an Anglican chapel). All its inhabitants lived in wooden cabins or houses, but only those residences and buildings belonging to the government (whether federal or provincial) or the mission had electricity. From fall 1966 Quaqtaq was linked to the outside world by radiotelephone and by a more or less regular mail service; the Quebec agent acted as both telephone operator and postmaster. Mail, light freight, and passengers were carried in and out

TABLE 3
Families Living in Quaqtaq, 15 August 1966

*Kindred A (husband/wife)*

| | |
|---|---|
| Saali/Miaji | Itittuuq/Qulliq |
| Jupi/Iiva | Jaiku/Lali |
| Ituaq/Sikuliaq | Ittuq/Nammaajuq |
| Inuppak (widow) | Uppik/Qupirruk |
| Ilaijja/Suusi | |

*Kindred B (husband/wife)*

| | |
|---|---|
| Matiusi/Aani Anautaq | Putulik/Luisa |
| Jaani (widower) | Aalupa/Suusi |

on flights operating from Kuujjuaq.[17] Bulkier materials were brought by ship during summer. There was no television, but most homes had transistor radios with which people were able to catch the Canadian Broadcasting Corporation's (CBC) short-wave northern service.

The settlement was very close-knit. All Quaqtaqmiut had near relatives living in the village. The core of the community consisted of a group of eight households (Kindred A;[18] see Table 3), formed by three siblings, their sister-in-law, her two married daughters, their uncle, and this uncle's married daughter. One more family was linked to this core, the wife being the adopted sister of the spouses of two of the siblings. These siblings were the children of Taqqiapik (died 1952) and Taqaq (died 1948), who had migrated to Tuvaaluk in 1940. Their uncle was Jaikuq, Taqqiapik's brother, who had himself moved to the area in 1941.

Another, smaller group (Kindred B) consisted of an older couple, their first cousin (a widower living with his unmarried sister), their married son, and this son's wife's brother. The wife and her brother were themselves first cousins to three persons belonging to the core group, with the consequence that all thirteen Quaqtaq households were related one to the other by kinship.

These kindreds were directly linked to the local bands that used to winter at Quaqtaq and Iggiajaq. Two children of Taqqiapik and one other member of the core group were married to Inuluk's offspring, and two members of Kindred B were the son and daughter of Nua Masik, the family head who had remained in Iggiajaq after his brother Inuluk's move to Quaqtaq.

In 1966–7 the main economic activities of Quaqtamiut still had much to do with hunting, fishing, and trapping. However, two recent technical innovations, the outboard motor canoe (*qajariaq*) and the snowmobile (skidoo; *sikiitu*), had greatly transformed the working conditions of the game harvesters, rendering them much more mobile and efficacious. These innovations sounded the demise of the kayak and dog team. The last kayak was seen once or twice during summer 1965, and after 1967 only a very few individuals kept any sled dogs, which they used for leisure (racing or taking foreign visitors out) rather than travel. The canoe and snowmobile also accelerated the decline of the spring camps because they enabled the men to reach their former hunting grounds rapidly and be back home at the village the same night or the next day. In June–July 1965 three families camped at Airartuuq and two at Salliq. The following year only three households left Quaqtaq during spring, none of them staying at Airartuuq.

As a consequence of these changes in the hunting and residence patterns, a growing number of women and children became confined within the precincts of the village. Whereas formerly the families had resided together at the various seasonal camps, now the men were the only ones to take part in hunting, trapping, or trading[19] expeditions. For most women and children the only possible outings were short fishing, shell-gathering, or berry-picking excursions in the vicinity of Quaqtaq, or visits to the Nuvuk weather station. One of the unexpected results of this situation was that the village was increasingly perceived to be a space where women were dominant. This explains at least partly why, over the following ten to fifteen years, the rate of female participation in community organizations was particularly high in Quaqtaq.

Despite these technological changes, the annual cycle of economic activities observed in 1966–7 was not that different from what it had been. In winter the men hunted seal at the edge of land-fast ice. They left in the morning, as soon as there was enough daylight, using their dog teams and snowmobiles to reach open water. A few hours later, when night began to fall, they came back.

Fox were scarce in the winter of 1965–6. The men did not bother to go trapping inland, being satisfied to set up a few traps around the village. Some women did likewise. The following winter (1966–7), however, fox were much more abundant. The trappers went inland by snowmobile once every two weeks to check their traps. In November and December 1966, ten men thus caught eighty animals. They travelled in rather large groups, their inland trapping expeditions giving them the opportunity to attend fishing nets set under the ice.

Hunting at the floe edge lasted until April. In May many hunters started going after seal basking on the Tuvaaluk ice, south of Quaqtaq. They usually departed for a few days at a time, by snowmobile or dog team, combining seal hunting with fishing. A few women took part in these expeditions. At the same time of the year, the men waited on shore for seal and beluga, at those locations where the ice had already broken up. This type of hunting was mainly conducted at Airartuuq, the hunters arriving from Quaqtaq in the morning and returning home at night. Some camped on the island for a couple of days, but none of the families who left the village during spring 1966 remained at Airartuuq.

Hunting from canoes began in late June. All summer long the men usually left with the day's first high tide, coming back ten to twelve hours later. Most of the time they went to the southern half of Tuvaaluk, where sea mammals were particularly numerous. Occasionally, they also hunted near Airartuuq. The canoes were used almost every day that weather and ice (in early summer) conditions allowed. From 25 June to 31 August 1966 there were thirty-eight days when at least one canoe was in use. On two occasions people went to Kangirsuk (a nine-hour trip under good conditions) by canoe.

Two Peterhead boats were in operation during the summer of 1966, each belonging to one of Quaqtaq's two kin groups. The first made seven hunting and fishing trips out of the village, but its captain was unable to form a stable crew. The other was manned by a more stable group of people, but it still went out only twice. Clearly, the Peterheads were suffering severe competition from canoes. In 1965, when the Quaqtamiut owned only six canoes, the three boats then in operation (see Appendix C) had respectively made seven, five, and four trips out of the village.

The canoes continued to be used during the fall of 1966, as long as the weather permitted. The men also hunted from the shore, in the vicinity of Quaqtaq. With the arrival of winter, in mid-November, they resumed trapping and hunting at the floe edge. As in the preceding periods, female activities were centred around the home. These included, for example, flensing, preparation of the skins, sewing, and cooking. Women were also active in trapping, fishing, and gathering, but it seems that sedentarization greatly restricted their participation in the collection of faunal resources.[20]

Trading activities continued to be the main source of income. Until the fall of 1966 only two full-time jobs were available to Quaqtaq Inuit, federal school janitor and maintenance worker at the Nuvuk weather station. With the construction of the DGNQ buildings, a third occupation appeared, that of provincial janitor. Most adults, however, had opportunities to work part time. The missionary hired five women to do his housekeeping. At the arrival of the supply ship, in July, the men received about $25 each for working as stevedores. Between September and December 1966, thirteen men laboured on the construction of the Quebec buildings, for an average pay of $485 per worker. This income was supplemented by transfer payments from the government, namely, family allowances, old age benefits, and direct relief.

Quaqtamiut were thus well conversant with cash economy, even if most of their activities still had to do with traditional pursuits. The village was also becoming acquainted with politics. On 2 January 1966 the federal teacher held a ballot to elect a three-man community council. The person chosen as chair was Jupi, one of the siblings belonging to Quaqtaq's core family group. The first councillor was his brother-in-law, Ituaq; the second, Miinnguq, was unrelated to the core group but chosen for his eloquence. Miinnguq moved out of Quaqtaq in May, and therefore another election was held in November. This time, Ituaq became president, Jupi first councillor, and his brother, Saali, second councillor.

These elections formalized leadership tendencies long latent within the community. As sons and son-in-law of the late Taqqiapik, Jupi, Saali, and Ituaq commanded central positions within Quaqtaq's principal kin group. Ituaq owned a Peterhead boat, and he and Jupi acted as Anglican catechists (lay readers), directing the weekly prayer services for the great majority of the population.[21] Both had succeeded their own fathers (Inuluk and Taqqiapik) in this position of spiritual leaders of the community, a fact which contributed to better entrench their authority. Modern politics thus continued to express social relations based on tradition.

The council's authority, however, remained strictly informal, with the elected body possessing no effective power. The teacher consulted its members from time to time, but all decisions concerning the administration and development of Quaqtaq were taken in Ottawa and Quebec or, to a lesser extent, by the Kuujjuaq federal NSO. Nobody was ready to listen to what Quaqtamiut had to say about their own community. Even the official name of the village, Koartak in English, Koartac[22] in French, was somewhat different from the original Inuit Quaqtaq.

The form of modernity into which Quaqtamiut and other Nunavik people had entered in 1966–7 thus seemed to require adoption of the Qallunaat way of life, as well as an almost complete dependence on the political will of the southern governments. Money economy, bureaucratic administration, and English-language education appeared as permanent fixtures of the new order of things. Many specialists (Jenness 1964, for instance) were persuaded that, to survive in this modern world, the Inuit had to forfeit their own culture and adopt that of the majority Canadians.

Despite appearances, however, Inuit identity remained quite strong. In Quaqtaq at the end of the 1960s hunting–gathering activities still constituted the mainstay of the economy, thus preserving an enduring relationship with the natural environment. Political decisions were taken by external agents, but, as we have seen, the internal functioning of the community continued to be based on kinship ties and cooperation among families. And finally, even if since 1960 school was taught exclusively in English, Inuktitut remained Quaqtaq's dominant language. Only one or two adults knew English at all, and outside the classroom, school-aged children always spoke Inuktitut.

## A Village under the James Bay Agreement

This sense of identity may explain why, during the 1970s, Quaqtamiut and other Nunavik Inuit, far from assimilating into the dominant culture, developed an entirely new way of relating to the rest of the world. Instead of becoming 'average Canadians,' as the bureaucrats had envisioned, they established their own economic, political, cultural, and educational organizations.

### Development and Municipalization

Between 1959 and 1962 the establishment of cooperatives in Puvirnituq (Povungnituk), Kangiqsualujjuaq (George River), and other settlements, had shown the Nunavik people that they were well able to manage by themselves businesses serving their particular needs and interests. The cooperative movement gave dozens upon dozens of men and women a basic training in Arctic economics and politics. This, combined with the graduation from high school, around 1970, of a first generation of young bilingual (Inuktitut–English) Inuit, made possible the advent of leaders well conversant in Qallunaat ways, but devoted to the promotion of aboriginal rights (see Crowe 1979).

The event that would completely transform the political and social organization of the Nunavik people occurred in 1971: Premier Robert Bourassa of Quebec declared that his government would develop the hydroelectric potential of several of the province's northern rivers. Cree and Inuit residents of the territory earmarked for development had not been consulted at all. When the first bulldozers began to actually plow the land, east of James Bay, their reaction was immediate. They asked a court to enjoin that all work stop at once, and this request was granted. To be able to go on with its megaproject, the Quebec government was thus forced to enter into negotiations with Arctic Quebec's aboriginal peoples.

Inuit were represented by the recently created Northern Quebec Inuit Association (NQIA). Three years of arduous negotiations finally led, on 11 November 1975, to the signing of the James Bay and Northern Quebec Agreement (*Angiqatigiinniq* 'the fact of agreeing together'), by which the Cree and Inuit renounced any further claim to the territory they occupied, in exchange for monetary compensations, the ownership and/or use of various tracts of land, and the establishment of a complete set of aboriginal organizations. As far as Inuit were concerned, these included an agency for economic development (the Makivik Corporation), a regional administration (the Kativik Regional Government or KRG), municipal councils in most communities,[23] a regional school board with extended powers in the fields of language use, teacher training, and curriculum development (the Kativik School Board), and various other boards and organizations dealing with, among other things, environmental problems and the delivery of health care.

Quaqtamiut did not play any active part in the negotiation and implementation of the agreement. They did not reject it either, being seemingly in agreement with most of its provisions. When the numerous boards and committees it provided for were established, the Quaqtaq people dutifully elected representatives to each of them, but they never took any leadership in the governance of Nunavik. Apart from a few local teachers active within various Kativik School Board task forces, only one local man, who has sat on the Kativik Consultative Committee on the Environment since its inception, may be said to have had some impact on regional policy making.

As in the rest of Nunavik, the James Bay Agreement brought much change to Quaqtaq, though the old order of things had begun to crumble earlier. Summer 1967 had seen the closing of the Roman Catholic mission, an institution that had contributed much, during the two decades of its existence, to the sedentarization of Tuvaalummiut. In September of the same year Quebec's DGNQ had opened a Kindergarten where teaching was conducted in Inuktitut, the teacher being a Qallunaaq woman who communicated with the children through interpreters.

In 1971 the Nuvuk weather station, Tuvaaluk's oldest surviving Euro-

Canadian establishment (it dated back to 1928), closed definitively, the equipment being moved to Quaqtaq, where a local resident was entrusted with sending weather reports. The advent of satellite telephone a few years later greatly improved communication between the village and the outside world.

During the second half of the 1960s health care had become a provincial responsibility in eastern Nunavik. A small hospital was built in Kuujjuaq and all villages were progressively allocated a resident nurse. Quaqtaq received its first nurse in 1972. She provided first aid care and supervised the evacuation of more seriously ill patients to the Kuujjuaq hospital or to a Montreal or Quebec City institution. One of the major consequences of this situation was that babies were now routinely delivered by the Kuujjuaq doctor rather than at home, by a local midwife. The ritual link between the newborn child and his or her midwife (*arnaquti* or *sanaji*) was thus severed, though some parents continued to ask an older woman to act as their child's symbolic midwife, even if the baby was born in the hospital.

These changes were merely the prelude to the deep-reaching transformations brought to the community by the James Bay Agreement. At the time the agreement was signed Quaqtamiut still had almost no say in the administration of their village. The community council remained purely consultative, and most local institutions, including the two schools,[24] continued to be directly run by the federal or provincial governments. Two organizations only, the store (which had become a cooperative in 1973) and the Anglican church, were in the hands of the local people.

The James Bay Agreement provided Inuit with various means of ensuring for themselves some measure of economic and administrative autonomy. Within a few years (i.e., between the signing of the agreement in 1975 and its implementation in 1977–8), what may be dubbed the benevolent dictatorship of the federal and provincial bureaucrats was replaced by an administrative apparatus consisting in several boards, corporations, and other organizations, whose directors were democratically elected by the population. It could be argued that traditional bureaucracy was replaced by a new one made up – in various proportions – of young educated Inuit and 'enlightened' Qallunaat sensitive to aboriginal rights.

In Quaqtaq the agreement was apparently accepted without any discussion. Quaqtamiut became the collective owners of a few dozen square kilometres of land, in and around the village (Category I lands, in the agreement's language), and they were recognized as having exclusive rights of use over a much larger territory (Category II lands) that covered much of their traditional hunting, fishing, and trapping grounds. These lands were to be managed by a local landholding corporation, the Tuvaaluk Corporation.

Various committees (e.g., land use, education, health and social services, and recreation) were set up in the village, and Quaqtamiut started sending representatives to the main regional organizations, including the Makivik Corporation, Kativik Regional Government, Kativik School Board, and Kativik Health and Social Services Regional Council. In 1978 the Kativik School Board took exclusive charge of formal education, and a young local woman, Lisi (Lizzie) Ningiuruvik, became head teacher of the Quaqtaq school.

The James Bay Agreement stipulated that the Nunavik communities would become full-fledged municipalities under a supramunicipal administration, the Kativik Regional Government (KRG). Accordingly, in 1980, Quaqtamiut elected their first mayor, Tivi Uppik (David Okpik), and six municipal councillors. A middle-aged woman, Iiva Taqqiapik (Eva Tukkiapik), was also chosen as Quaqtaq's representative to KRG.

Social and political development preceding the agreement or generated by it had a direct economic impact on the community. Several new jobs were created (e.g., in the municipal administration) and many occupations formerly held by transient Qallunaat (such as schoolteacher, weather station operator, store manager, and postmaster) were transferred to local people, as the federal and provincial governments progressively withdrew from direct involvement in the administration of Nunavik.

The increasing availability of jobs, coupled with family reunification, explains the population growth observed between 1967 and 1980. During this period, eleven families moved to Quaqtaq, while only two left the village.[25] Several of these migrations involved people living in Killiniq (Port Burwell), a village built on an island offshore from the Nunavik and Labrador coasts and belonging to the Northwest Territories.

In 1977 the federal government decided to close Killiniq, whose population had not ceased to decrease over the past ten years (see Dawson 1984). A former Quaqtamiuq named Kumak, who had migrated to Killiniq in 1962, then chose to move back to Quaqtaq with his wife and children. They had been preceded there by two of his siblings, as well as by his father-in-law. Kumak was accompanied by four families related to his wife. Most of these people were native Killinirmiut and northern Labradorians and had never been to Tuvaaluk before. They moved there because they had no place else to go.

*Quaqtaq in 1981*

At the end of May 1981 the population of Quaqtaq had more than doubled

TABLE 4
Families Living in Quaqtaq, 31 May 1981

*Kindred A (husband/wife)*

| | |
|---|---|
| Saali/Miaji | Itittuuq/Qulliq |
| Jupi/Iiva | Lali (widow) |
| Ituaq/Sikuliaq | Ittuq/Nammaajuq |
| Inuluk/Inugaluaq | Uppik/Qupirruk |
| Ilaijja/Suusi | Saaliattuk/Paasa |

*Kindred B (husband/wife)*

| | |
|---|---|
| Matiusi (widower) | Putulialuk/Kasitiina |
| Jaani (widower) | Papialuk Deer/Iiva |
| Putulik/Luisa | Pita Ningiuruvik/Lisi |
| Suusi (widow) | Aupaluk (bachelor) |

*Kindred C (husband/wife)*

| | |
|---|---|
| Minialuk (bachelor) | Uili/Iiva |
| Kumak/Iima | Suusi/Paulusi |
| Jaji Arnatuq (bachelor) | Pinijami Jararusi/Iimali |
| Iimali Qupanuaq (widow) | Michael Keelan/Suupi |

over the preceding fifteen years, with 158 Inuit and 9 Qallunaat residents.[26] The village area had also been multiplied by a factor of three or four. The public buildings now included a large school, a nursing station, a town hall, an office–residence for the Quebec agent, a cooperative store, two churches (Anglican and Pentecostal), and several other structures. A year-round landing strip, a fuel oil delivery complex, and an automated satellite telephone station completed the picture.

The Inuit population lived in twenty-six residences,[27] and the transient Qallunaat (two nurses and two teachers, with their dependents) occupied three additional houses. Most Quaqtamiut were related to each other by blood. The two groups of relatives observed in 1966 were still present. Both had expanded significantly, however, by immigration of new elements or through the marriage of their younger members. In 1981 the offspring of Taqqiapik and Taqaq and their kin comprised ten families (Kindred A; see Table 4), and the siblings and cousins who formed the other group (Kindred B) were now distributed among eight households. A third group

(Kindred C) had appeared since 1966. It included the loosely related families who had moved from Killiniq between 1969 and 1979. In 1981 these people formed eight households.

For many Quaqtamiut hunting and fishing activities remained very important. Weather permitting, from five to ten men left the village every day, by snowmobile or canoe, to go after seal, walrus, and beluga. Between February and April caribou were to be found a few dozen kilometres from the village, thus providing people with a resource that had been lacking in the preceding decades.

Eight out of thirty-five men over 18 years old considered themselves professional hunters. Without a regular job, they spent most of their time going after game. When weather was particularly good, however, the majority of the male wage workers temporarily left their work to join the others in pursuit of seal or caribou. Several young women were occasional hunters, a novelty over the preceding periods, when women almost never touched guns.

The purpose of these hunting activities was primarily commercial: selling sealskins and walrus ivory to the Quaqtaq cooperative or to the Kangirsuk HBC store. Without sled dogs to feed, the hunters did not need all the meat they caught. They thus only brought home what was necessary for human consumption. Daily meals still included much local food, though, a fact that contributed to reduce family spending.

In 1981 the hunting techniques had not changed very much from 1966: waiting for seal at the floe edge during winter, hunting seal and beluga from the shore in spring and fall, hunting from canoes during summer and early fall. The spring hunt for seal basking on the sea ice (*uuttuq*), however, had almost completely disappeared. Similarly, after the 1967 summer season, no Peterhead boat was used again, thus putting an end to team hunting.

Spring camps were still occasionally visited. In July 1981 three families spent two or three weeks at Airartuuq, and two other households stayed a month in Salliq. Interestingly enough, these people or their immediate relatives had already frequented these same two camps in the mid-1960s, camping having thus become a sort of family tradition for them.

All year long several Quaqtamiut went fishing with lines, nets, or three-pronged spears. Some fox trapping was undertaken, but this activity had lost most of its earlier importance. A few individuals set traps near the village, but it was too costly and too inconvenient for those holding regular jobs to leave Quaqtaq for two or three weeks, as had formerly been done. Most men went hunting and fishing alone or with an adolescent boy, generally related to them.

In 1981 meat and fish were still shared with relatives and friends, but surplus game was also sold to the cooperative, where anybody could buy it back. More generally, the consumption level of Quaqtamiut had increased tremendously since 1966–7. According to statistics released by Quebec's Department of Financial Institutions and Corporations (MIFC 1981), the population of Quaqtaq spent a total of $596,000 in 1980, an average of $22,096 for each family. Most of this sum (80.7 per cent) was used for buying various goods, only 4.3 per cent of it being spent on housing.

Naturally enough, this high level of consumption proceeded directly from increased income. The MIFC (1981) showed that in 1980 the total income of the Quaqtamiut amounted to $726,000, of which 75.1 per cent came from wages and other sources (e.g., the sale of furs) and 24.9 per cent from transfer payments, for example, family allowances, direct relief (5.6 per cent of the total income), and unemployment insurance benefits. The average family income for 1980 reached $26,907, an increase of more than 1700 per cent since 1966–7 (when it stood at $1500).

This stupendous growth in monetary returns was, above all, the result of the introduction of wage labour and of the general salary increases that followed the James Bay Agreement. In March 1980 twenty-five native Quaqtamiut held jobs in Quaqtaq, according to a Kativik Regional Government report (KRG 1980). In July 1981 twenty-seven individuals (sixteen men and eleven women) worked locally, and five more – all of them women – held jobs outside Quaqtaq. All these occupations had to do with the delivery of services. The biggest employer was the Kativik School Board (in 1981 it hired eleven persons from the village), followed by the municipal corporation (five workers, including the mayor), and by about ten other organizations. In addition, temporary work was occasionally available (e.g., on construction sites), in or outside Quaqtaq.

Since 1980 the village had been administered by a municipal council (comprising the mayor and six councillors), which supervised housing, road maintenance, water delivery, garbage removal, and so forth. In 1981 the mayor belonged to Quaqtaq's largest group of relatives (Kindred A), and his councillors were distributed among all three existing groups. People from Kindreds A and B (the latter in a lesser way), but not from Kindred C (the former Killinirmiut), also participated in the four or five local consultative committees. Women comprised about half of the Quaqtamiut involved in local or regional administration.

The most important organization was the school. It had hired eleven people, nine Inuit and two transient Qallunaat. Under the direction of its principal, Iiva (Eva) Deer, it served to the educational needs of all children. Teaching was in Inuktitut during the first three years (Kindergarten and

Grades 1 and 2). It then switched to English or French, according to the parents' choice, up to Secondary III (Grade 9). Children wishing to complete high school had to leave for Kuujjuaq, Montreal, or Quebec City.

Inuktitut was still spoken by the entire Inuit population, including the children of the two mixed couples. Television had not yet arrived,[28] but the school sometimes showed video cassettes in the native language. The village had its own FM radio transmitter, which broadcast music and local information and opinions several hours a day. A community hall belonging to the municipality was used for meetings, film shows, and occasional dances. Most households took part in these communal activities, whatever the kindred to which they belonged.

Religion was the only sphere where the subdivision into family groupings had become somewhat institutionalized. After the closing of the mission in 1967 the four Roman Catholics started to attend Anglican services, and for a few years the entire community practised the same religion. But in the mid-1970s the Pentecostal faith was brought to Quaqtaq.[29] This creed became so popular that in 1978 its adherents built a small church. In 1981 forty-three Quaqtamiut (27 per cent of the native population) were Pentecostals. All of them belonged to Kindred B, the members of the two other family groups remaining Anglicans. In a symbolic way, this kindred's religious autonomy counterbalanced its poor participation in Quaqtaq's various councils and committees.

Spurred by the Pentecostal challenge, the Anglicans renewed some of their practices. They established a women's committee, rebuilt their church, and started to offer Bible courses. The village did not have the benefit of an ordained minister, but the training of local catechists improved.

In the early years of the James Bay Agreement, Quaqtamiut thus seemed endowed with all the trappings of modernity. Wage labour, an extensive administrative structure, and new – or renovated – religious ideas now dominated. Like other Inuit, the Quaqtaq people had gained better access to money, formal education, and modern technology. But at the same time, they remained genuine Inuit. Their native identity was principally supported by their hunting and fishing activities – still important despite the development of wage work – and by their daily use of the Inuktitut language. In the next chapters, I shall describe in more detail this ongoing interaction between modernity and identity.

# 3

# Quaqtaq in the 1990s

Over a period of some forty years (1940–80) Quaqtaq evolved from a winter camp to a fully sedentarized village. Concurrently, its social organization became increasingly complex. Local bands who harvested their territory's fauna through a well-adjusted seasonal cycle of hunting, fishing, trapping, and gathering activities, progressively became family groupings whose members competed for wage-earning occupations and for positions within a diversified political and administrative structure. The culture of the Tuvaaluk Inuit would seem to have been drowned by a host of exogenous concepts and living habits introduced through the school, the media, and increased contact with the outside world.

By 1990, then, Quaqtamiut were quite familiar with modernity. They did not have much cause to envy their southern compatriots in terms of technical development, economic opportunities, and educational facilities. Meanwhile, they continued to preserve their uniqueness and specific identity. We shall now examine this apparent paradox – the survival of identity within modernity, starting with a description of some physical and organizational characteristics of Quaqtaq in the early 1990s.[1]

## Physical Setting

Seen from the air, Quaqtaq looks like a tiny coloured dot, engulfed, in winter, within the ubiquitous whiteness of the snow-covered land- and seascape. The village stands on the shore of a little cove that opens widely on the northeastern portion of Tuvaaluk (see Map 2). This cove is somewhat sheltered from the prevailing winds by a one-kilometre long promontory called Nuvukutaaq ('the long point'), which extends on its northern side. Tuvaaluk's biggest island, Qikirtaaluk, lies directly across from the mouth of the cove, and it also partly contributes to shelter the village from storms and blizzards.

MAP 3
Quaqtaq in 1990

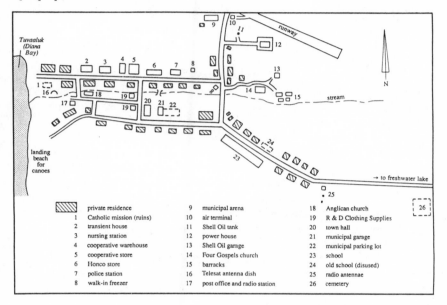

| | | | | | |
|---|---|---|---|---|---|
| | private residence | 9 | municipal arena | 18 | Anglican church |
| 1 | Catholic mission (ruins) | 10 | air terminal | 19 | R & D Clothing Supplies |
| 2 | transient house | 11 | Shell Oil tank | 20 | town hall |
| 3 | nursing station | 12 | power house | 21 | municipal garage |
| 4 | cooperative warehouse | 13 | Shell Oil garage | 22 | municipal parking lot |
| 5 | cooperative store | 14 | Four Gospels church | 23 | school |
| 6 | Honco store | 15 | barracks | 24 | old school (disused) |
| 7 | police station | 16 | Telesat antenna dish | 25 | radio antennae |
| 8 | walk-in freezer | 17 | post office and radio station | 26 | cemetery |

On the ground Quaqtaq appears as a small agglomeration extending lon-
gitudinally along a shallow valley bordered by low hills. Its shore is rocky,
except for a sandy beach situated just south of the built-up section. In summer this beach is used as a landing place for canoes and boats, despite the
reefs and shoals that make access difficult at low tide. The village is bisected
by a narrow stream that runs along its length and empties into the cove.

Quaqtaq's unpaved streets form a rough quadrangle whose two long
sides parallel the stream (see Map 3). Northward from the village a road
leads to the airport and to the municipal dump. Southeast of the quadrangle
the street running on the south side of the stream extends into a two-
kilometre route that reaches the small lake used as the community's water
supply. Quaqtaq's main cemetery lies on a hill along this road.

The village saw much physical development in the 1980s. Around 1986
most existing houses were replaced by larger and better ones, and new residences were built. On 1 June 1990 Quaqtaq had forty one-family dwellings
(as compared with twenty-nine in 1981), plus two apartment buildings
accommodating six households each. Additional residences were built in
August and September of that same year.[2] All these houses are now

equipped with a flush toilet and hot and cold running water, and a few are two storeys high. The residences of the Inuit belong to the Société d'habitation du Québec, the Quebec government's housing authority, which rents them to Quaqtamiut through a locally elected housing committee. The rent, which includes electricity and heating, is proportional to the dwellers' monthly income.

In addition to these private residences, Quaqtaq has a score of public buildings. The most prominent of these is the school, rebuilt in the 1980s, whose gymnasium doubles as a community hall. Important also is the town hall, which stands right in the middle of the village, flanked by a garage and parking lot for municipal vehicles. Other buildings include the nursing station, a small police station, a guest house for visitors, the landholding corporation's (Tuvaaluk Corporation) office, a municipal walk-in freezer, and a structure housing the post office and the community radio station.[3] Two churches, one at each end of the village, are also to be found: the Anglican church and the Four Gospels Pentecostal prayer house.[4]

Quaqtaq now has three commercial buildings: the cooperative store; Honco Inc., a subsidiary of the landholding corporation selling hunting gear, tools, and motor parts; and a privately owned clothing and sundry store (R. & D. Clothing Supplies). A small service zone lies northeast of the village. It comprises the Hydro-Québec power plant, the Shell Oil fuel and gasoline tanks and pumps, and a few barracks occasionally used by construction workers. Further from the village is the airport and, across the street from the terminal, the municipal hockey arena. Both were opened in 1989.

The physical development of the community is partly the result of its demographic growth. On 1 January 1991 Quaqtaq's population reached 235, a marked increase from 1981, when it stood at 167. The vast majority of Quaqtamiut were permanent residents: 225 individuals, including 219 Inuit and six non-Inuit men married to local women.[5] There were only ten transient Qallunaat: two nurses, five teachers, and their three dependents.

Among the Inuit, women were a little more numerous (112) than men (107), for a sex ratio (number of men/number of women) of 0.96. The lower numbers of men were particularly noticeable among those born between 1931 and 1935 (i.e., aged between 55 and 59 on 1 January 1991), who counted only two men, against seven women. This was undoubtedly the result of a higher mortality (partly caused by hunting and travel accidents) among the men, though in the next age group (people 60 years old and over), there were as many men (three) as there were women (see Table 5).

Some migrations occurred between 1981 and 1991, but the demographic

TABLE 5
Resident Population by Sex and Age, Quaqtaq, 1 January 1991

| Age (Years) | Male | Female | Total |
|---|---|---|---|
| ≥60 | 3 | 3 | 6 |
| 55–9 | 2 | 7 | 9 |
| 50–4 | 2 | 2 | 4 |
| 45–9 | 2 | 1 | 3 |
| 40–4 | 3 | 3 | 6 |
| 35–9 | 5 | 3 | 8 |
| 30–4 | 9 | 9 | 18 |
| 25–9 | 14 | 10 | 24 |
| 20–4 | 9 | 13 | 22 |
| 15–19 | 10 | 13 | 23 |
| 10–14 | 11 | 14 | 25 |
| 5–9 | 21 | 17 | 38 |
| 0–4 | 22 | 17 | 39 |
| Total | 113 | 112 | 225 |
| Inuit residents | 107 | 112 | 219 |
| Non-Inuit residents | 6 | 0 | 6 |

increase was principally the result of the natural growth of the population. Most migratory movements involved families of the former Killinirmiut. A few persons migrated individually (or with a young child) to join with a potential spouse in Quaqtaq[6] or, in a few cases, to marry outside the Tuvaaluk area.[7] In the 1980s, however, most unions involved two individuals already living in the village. The younger members of Kindred C (the former Killinirmiut) thus had the opportunity, through marriage with local girls, to become fully integrated into the community.

On 1 January 1991 the 225 permanent residents of Quaqtaq were distributed among fifty different households, including twelve one-person residential units (see Figure 1). The majority of these households (twenty-four of fifty) belonged to Kindred A (the offspring and other relatives of Taqqiapik and Taqaq), which still remained the major kin group within the community.[8] Sixteen more households belonged to Kindred B, and six to Kindred C. Four young families were headed by a couple whose husband

# FIGURE 1
Kinship Relations among the Resident Households, Quaqtaq, January 1991

## Kindred A

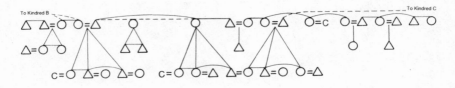

## Kindred B

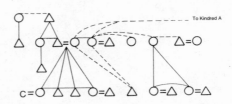

## Kindred C

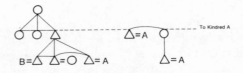

**Symbols**                                    **Household heads**

|   | parent-child relation | △ | single/widowed male |
| sibling relation | | ○ | single/widowed female |
| other relation (in-law, nephew, cousin) | | △=○ | married couple (A-B-C: spouse from another kindred) |

was from Kindred C, but whose wife came from Kindreds A (three cases) or B (one case). Interestingly enough, there were no unions between members of Kindreds A and B, a fact that stresses the persistence of intra-community social boundaries.

Table 5 shows the distribution of Quaqtaq's permanent residents by sex and age groups. This is a very young population. On 1 January 1991 a third (34 per cent) of all Quaqtamiut were under 10 years of age, 45 per cent under 15, and 55.5 per cent under 20. By contrast, some age groups were particularly thin. Only six persons (2.6 per cent of the total) between 40 and 44 years old, three (1.3 per cent) between 45 and 49, and four (1.8 per cent) between 50 and 54 were to be found. These individuals had been born during the very difficult period surrounding the Second World War, and their small numbers surely reflect the high mortality caused by the economic and health problems that prevailed then.

Another peculiarity that Table 5 reveals is the unequal distribution of males and females in the younger age groups. For example, more boys (twenty-one) than girls (seventeen) are aged between 5 and 9, but more girls (fourteen) than boys (eleven) are between 10 and 14. This discrepancy is most probably the result of chance. When all Quaqtamiut under 25 are lumped together, they yield a more balanced ratio of seventy-three males for seventy-four females.

## Economic Activities

The people of Quaqtaq remain very much involved in hunting and fishing. These activities, however, are not lucrative enough to enable them to earn a living, and wage labour plays a most important part in their economic life. As a matter of fact, traditional pursuits now provide returns that are proportionally lower in Quaqtaq than in many other Nunavik communities.

### Hunting, Fishing, and Trapping

In 1990 only eight men, out of fifty-one male Quaqtamiut aged 19 years old and over, devoted the major part of their working time to hunting and fishing. A ninth, born in 1916, had hunted and trapped all his life, but was now too old to leave the village. Despite demographic growth, then, the number of game and fish harvesters did not increase between 1981 and 1990. The three younger men who became full-time hunters in this period barely replaced those who retired or died. As in 1981, however, most male Quaqtamiut still availed themselves of every opportunity to go out hunting during their spare time. Moreover, as we shall see later on, life on the land now also involved women and children.

The Quaqtaq area remains what it has always been: a promontory surrounded by waters noted for their abundance of game. Moreover, adjacent land is now teeming with caribou. Quaqtamiut take advantage of this abundance in many ways. Most male wage workers go hunting every Saturday,[9] weather permitting, and between May and August some of them also hunt after work, availing themselves of the long hours of daylight that characterize spring and summer. A few women are occasional hunters, but the pursuit of game remains predominantly an activity of men.

In contrast with 1981, when hunting primarily served commercial purposes, people now mainly hunt for food. Seal and caribou skins are worth almost nothing (sealskins were bought for some $3 apiece in 1993), a situation for which many Quaqtamiut blame ecological groups such as Greenpeace (on this topic, see Lynge 1992). The men therefore go after animals to procure fresh meat. Besides seal, beluga, and caribou, they hunt migratory birds (principally in the spring and fall). In the appropriate seasons, people also gather shellfish (mainly clams and mussels), eggs, eider-down, and berries. But even if food from the land still constitutes the main source of proteins, the community's needs are somewhat limited, with the result that for most individuals, hunting expeditions are less frequent (once a week instead of every day) than they used to be twenty-five or thirty years ago. The government also imposes quotas on some species (e.g., polar bear and beluga), which further restricts hunting possibilities.

These circumstances partly explain why fishing has recently gained in importance. Whereas formerly the basic diet consisted of seal and beluga meat (together with bannock – a pan-fried bread – and tea), it now mainly comprises fish (principally arctic char) and caribou. Interestingly enough, the latter foodstuffs are precisely those that are preferred by Qallunaat. In addition to ecological and economic factors, acculturation in culinary tastes might thus also account for the changes in diet observed over recent decades.

Fishing is particularly in favour among women and younger persons. Most of Quaqtaq's adult females mention this activity as their principal occupation outside domestic and wage work. In spring and late summer, many women go fishing once a week, often spending two or three days at a time out of the village. Fishing also occurs during fall and winter. Some women – along with a few younger men – are involved in trapping, but this activity remains marginal. In the old days it was the only way to earn money, which is clearly not the case any more. Thus, people do not bother to spend much time and energy on catching fox, even if the price of skins is relatively high (around $20 apiece in March 1993).

Many individuals, especially among younger people, are barred from pursuing land activities by the prohibitive cost of hunting gear and motorized vehicles. For example, it costs some $15,000 to buy a snowmobile and use it for two or three seasons. Despite the fact that hunters are subsidized by the government, it often happens that to buy and maintain the material required for land activities, one must hold a wage-earning position. Most unemployed individuals may only expect to borrow occasionally the snowmobile or canoe of a more affluent relative or friend.

For Quaqtamiut, hunting, fishing, and trapping are much more than mere economic pursuits. They symbolize a way of life closely related to Inuit identity. Many men and women state that, apart from being an opportunity to get access to fresh food, these activities help them keep contact with traditional culture. They also constitute occasions to transmit this culture to their young. Accordingly, some older hunters invite adolescents and young men to accompany them, to teach them how to live on the land. A few youngsters, however, deplore that this does not happen often enough, stating that many elders do not seem very eager to transmit their knowledge.

Many families have now built themselves cabins at various hunting and fishing sites (e.g., Airartuuq and Tasirjuakuluk). All through the year, parents and children travel to these for a few days at a time to undertake traditional activities. On these occasions children learn a lot about life on the land. They hunt, fish, and trap with their elders, and many of them eat otherwise unavailable foods, such as *igunaq* (gamy meat) or *puurtaq* (meat kept in a sealskin pouch until it becomes 'high').

The building of permanent cabins caused the almost complete disappearance of traditional spring camps. Camp life is now possible all year-round, because most people, whatever their sex and age, have access to their own hunting and fishing cottages, or to those of their relatives. This does not mean that all sites are accessible at all seasons. Obviously, the inland locations (including Tasirjuakuluk) can only be reached when the snow cover is sufficient to allow travel by snowmobile. But all through the year, some good fishing and hunting grounds, where relatively comfortable accommodations can be found, are within reach of Quaqtamiut.

This new way of living on the land was made possible by the acquisition of faster and more reliable means of transportation. Almost all Quaqtaq households have one or two snowmobiles, and most of them also have a canoe or motorboat, and, sometimes, an all-terrain wheeled vehicle. Two longliners[10] and one smaller boat are to be found in the community. One longliner belongs to the landholding corporation, which uses it for collective hunting, fishing, and trading expeditions. The other two boats are privately owned.

Thus, travelling has become easier than it used to be. Women and younger people now travel by themselves (i.e., without adult male companions) to the fishing and hunting grounds. Because of their relative lack of experience, this is not without risks. Navigational aids have therefore been installed, including wooden poles that mark the winter snowmobile trail between Tasirjuakuluk and the south shore of Tuvaaluk.

Hunting, fishing, and trapping are partly subsidized by the Quebec government. In December 1982 a provincial law established a program whereby the Nunavik municipalities would receive grants aimed at purchasing equipment, reducing the cost of gasoline, and buying surplus meat, fish, and other land products from the hunters and fishers. This law seems to have yielded good results because even some younger individuals (those in the 15 to 19 age group) are participating in the program (Duhaime 1990).

When somebody comes back with meat, fish, or skins, he or she may sell part of his or her catch to the municipality, at a price fixed by the village council. In March 1993, for example, the Quaqtaq council bought caribou meat at $1 per pound. The products thus purchased are stored in the municipal freezer, where they are available free of charge to anybody in need.

This institutionalized distribution system has not replaced more traditional sharing patterns. In Quaqtaq people still share food from the land with their relatives. They consider sharing (*ningirsiniq*) and mutual aid (*ikajuutiniq*) to be fundamental characteristics of Inuit culture and identity. Many Quaqtamiut state that one should not only help his or her own family, but also anybody in need. Some add that this is required by both traditional custom and religion. According to many, the Inuit way of life is characterized by the fact that people help their neighbours without having to be asked to do so. Generally speaking, then, Quaqtamiut view their culture as based on community-wide cooperation, although most of them state that such cooperation is on the decrease.

*Wage Labour and Business*

The cultural importance of land activities, sharing, and mutual aid does not preclude Quaqtamiut from being fully involved in the modern labour market. As a matter of fact, the major part of their income is drawn from wage work and business. Hunting and trapping revenues now constitute only a negligible percentage of their total monetary earnings.

According to the 1991 Canadian census, 62.5 per cent of all Quaqtaq residents and transients aged between 15 and 65 were active in the labour force in 1990. Those who held a job or were actively seeking one included a higher percentage of men (72.7 per cent) than of women (61.5 per cent), but among the actual job holders (sixty-five individuals, or 83 per cent of all active persons), there were more women (thirty-five) than men (thirty).

In June 1990 I identified forty-two resident Quaqtamiut (twenty men and twenty-two women) and seven transients (two men and five women) holding a full-time occupation. In regard to census data this means that there were about sixteen individuals whom I did not list as wage workers, but who were nevertheless deriving some income from various sources, such as participation in one or the other of the local committees, part-time construction work, or occasional stevedoring or snowplowing chores.

All forty-nine full-time job holders worked in the services sector, including education, health, administration, utilities, transportation, and retail trade. Only two owned their business, the balance being employees. Many jobs changed hands quite often, and nobody seemed really interested to remain in the same occupation for the rest of his or her life. Several individuals acted as substitute workers, replacing a job holder when he or she was absent from the village.

As had been the case in 1981, the biggest employer was the Kativik School Board, which hired nineteen persons, including twelve teachers (seven Inuit and five transient Qallunaat). The next largest job provider was the municipality, with seven regular employees working either in the office or on the maintenance and water delivery crews. It was followed by the nursing station, which hired six persons: two transient Qallunaat nurses and four local helpers (including a resident Qallunaaq).

Five individuals worked for private businesses including the R & D Clothing Supplies store owner (a resident non-Inuk), his salesclerk, the Shell concessionnaire, and Shell's two employees. The cooperative provided two full-time jobs, those of manager and cashier. Ten more people were hired by half a dozen other employers.

On the whole, then, in 1990 thirty-eight full-time occupations (including those of mayor and school principal, municipal secretary, cooperative manager, teacher, policeman, and Shell Oil concessionnaire) where held by Quaqtaq Inuit, and eleven by non-Inuit (four of them being residents and seven transients). Women were mainly to be found in white-collar jobs (e.g., mayor and school principal, teacher, and interpreter), whereas the majority of men were blue-collar workers.

Many Quaqtamiut feel that all positions within the village could and should be occupied by Inuit, often giving the example of the municipal administration and services, which are entirely run by native individuals. They state that employment is a major problem for young people, and that the creation of jobs should be given absolute priority. They resent the fact that some Qallunaat took advantage of their higher level of formal schooling – or, in one case, appealed to Quebec's Commission on Human Rights – to get hold of occupations which had, up to then, been occupied by Inuit.

A few individuals have established their own business. Quaqtaq's oldest private concern is Shell Oil Inc. Since the mid-1970s the Shell concession has partly belonged to a local Inuk resident, who is in charge of selling and distributing gasoline and fuel oil brought to Quaqtaq once a year by ship. Another commercial venture, the clothing and sundries store (known as R & D Clothing Supplies), has been in operation since the late 1980s. It belongs to a long-time non-Inuk resident. Besides his store, this entrepreneur owns one of Quaqtaq's two longliner boats. In the summer of 1992, with a crew of three men, he started a scallop fishery in Tuvaaluk's waters. If a large enough market is found, this fishery might develop over the years.

In 1990 at least three individuals operated micro-businesses at home. Two of them rented video cassettes, and a third sold beauty products. On top of that, the radio station offered bracelets and earrings for sale. One man contemplated organizing sled and dog-team expeditions for tourists. In collaboration with a southern travel agency, nine-day package tours were actually offered during the 1992 winter season, but they only attracted a handful of visitors.

Quaqtaq's main trading establishment is the cooperative store. It offers a limited selection of food items, clothing, houseware, and general merchandise. It also buys skins from the hunters and trappers. Fishing and hunting gear, construction material, tools, and motor parts can be bought from Honco Inc., the landholding corporation's (Tuvaaluk) store. Boats and snowmobiles may also be ordered through this outlet. As they have always done, Quaqtamiut also get supplied from outside the community. They still patronize Kangirsuk's former HBC trading post, which now belongs to the Northern Stores chain, and they often order merchandise – by phone, fax, or mail – from southern concerns. Trips 'down south,' whether for business, pleasure, or health care, also constitute occasions to obtain otherwise unavailable items.

With an approximate annual family income of $35,800 in 1991,[11] Quaqtamiut now have an enviable buying power, especially when one considers that housing, gasoline, and food from the land are well subsidized. There are some discrepancies in income among the families, but these are not always apparent. With sharing and mutual aid patterns still in force, no big differences between rich and poor people can as yet be found in Quaqtaq. In the economic sphere, then, modernity and identity seem to be getting along relatively well.

## Community Organizations

Administration is another sphere where modernity and identity appear to cohabit smoothly. The James Bay Agreement provided the Nunavik communities with a very complete set of local and regional organizations, whose stated objective is to improve the native population's participation in its own administration. As was already the case in 1981, Quaqtamiut today belong to several councils and committees that oversee various aspects of public life. Even if they seldom play a major role at the national or regional level, they surely are very active on the local scene.

Quaqtaq's principal administrative body is the municipal council, which comprises a mayor and six councillors, elected every two years. The council's responsibilities include road maintenance, garbage disposal, and the distribution of water. The municipality also deals with more specialized tasks like buying food from the land and storing it in the community freezer (see preceding section); allotting houses to those who need them; and supervising the hockey arena and the local radio station. The mayor belongs to the Kativik Regional Government, a supralocal body serving the administration of the whole of Nunavik.

In 1990 Quaqtaq's mayor, Eva Deer, was a woman in her early forties belonging to Kindred B. She had replaced another woman, a member of Kindred A, who had intermittently held the mayorship between 1983 and 1989. In 1991 she was succeeded by an older man, David Okpik, Quaqtaq's first mayor, who belonged to Kindred A. But Deer regained power in 1993.

Contrary to their predecessor, a housewife who spoke only Inuktitut, Eva Deer and David Okpik both belong to the first generation of Quaqtamiut who learned English and worked for Qallunaat organizations, while being at the same time fully involved in the new administrative bodies provided for by the James Bay Agreement. Deer acts as school principal and, since the early 1980s, as community representative to the Makivik Corporation's board of directors. Okpik sits on the Kativik Consultative

Committee on the Environment. Both of them thus combine traditional knowledge – having lived in camps during their youth – with linguistic and administrative skills relevant to their function.

In 1990 the members of the municipal council – three men and three women aged between 30 and 65 – belonged to Kindreds A (four individuals) and B (two individuals, including a resident non-Inuk). Three councillors spoke only Inuktitut. Two were teachers, two businessmen, and two primarily oriented towards traditional land activities. Except for members of Kindred C and of the younger generation, all of Quaqtaq's gender, age, kinship, and economic groupings were thus represented on the council.

As far as gender is concerned, it should be mentioned here that many outsiders, whether Inuit or Qallunaat, consider Quaqtaq to be a place where power lies in the hands of the women. It is true that during the 1980s, many committees – including at times the municipal council – were exclusively female in their composition. When questioned about the participation of women in local politics and administration, Quaqtamiut generally answer that people belonging to both sexes try to help each other in running the village properly, and that they do not perceive any predominance of one gender over the other.

In their eyes, the municipality's hold on local power is perfectly legitimate, even if they may criticize one or the other of the particular mayors or councillors. The municipal council votes numerous by-laws and regulations, whose written version is posted in strategic locations. Some people complain – albeit jokingly – that in Quaqtaq everything is now regulated by law, but, generally speaking, they abide by the spirit – if not always the letter – of the regulations voted by the council.

One of the most important municipal institutions is the hockey arena, a covered building built and opened in 1989. Its ice is natural and it can therefore only operate during the winter months. The arena is used for both leisure skating and hockey games. In a village where organized activities are few, it provides a welcome locale for community-wide encounters. At the same time it contributes to fostering a common identity for all Quaqtamiut.

In season, hockey games are held every day except Sunday. There are two major teams, both exclusively male, the Icebergs and the Old Timers. The first comprises adolescents and young adults, whereas the second is made up of men over 30 years of age. These two teams regularly compete against each other, and they also participate in Ungava-wide or Nunavik-wide hockey tournaments. Besides the Icebergs and Old Timers, there are several informal teams for schoolchildren (boys and girls) and women.

Each team – including the two main ones – comprises players belonging to all three kindreds. Hockey thus contributes to mix the various family groups. Community spirit and identity are also reinforced when the Icebergs or Old Timers play against neighbouring villages. In Quaqtaq everybody seems to love hockey, and this sport must be considered as playing a central part in the life of the community.

Another important institution is the local FM radio station (*tusauti* 'the listening instrument'). Its technical equipment belongs to Taqramiut Nipingat Inc., an Inuit broadcasting organization based in Salluit, but it is managed by the municipality. In 1990 it could be heard for seven hours a day, broadcasting a mix of CBC Northern Service programs and local content. The latter consisted of Inuit and Qallunaat taped music, interspersed with community or personal announcements. Everybody was welcome to phone the station to air his or her own message, which ran from the trivial ('so-and-so is required by his or her parents to come home for lunch') to the expression of strong opinions on various topics. Quaqtaq's *tusauti* thus enabled the entire community to play an active role in the transmission of local information.

Although the municipality serves the administrative needs of the village, the land itself is owned and managed by a holding corporation (*nunamik tigumiartikut* 'those who hold the land'), Tuvaaluk Corporation, which has its own board of directors, elected by the local beneficiaries of the James Bay Agreement. In 1993 it was chaired by the owner of R & D Clothing Supplies. The corporation operates a longliner boat, as well as the Honco Inc. store. It also supervises land allotment, hunting licences, and, through the Shell concessionnaire (Qalluti Inc.), the distribution of fuel oil and gasoline.

Besides its municipal government, Quaqtaq's most important organization is the Isummasaqvik ('the place where one seeks to understand') School. Built in the mid-1980s, the school is an imposing building with several fully equipped classrooms, ample office space, and a huge gymnasium where the entire population of the village can gather together.[12] Its general management, including the hiring of teachers, is under the responsibility of a five-member local education committee. Quaqtamiut also send an elected representative to the Kativik School Board's Council of Commissioners.

Nineteen persons worked for the school during the 1989–90 academic year. There were sixty-seven students (30 per cent of the resident population), in seven classes. The school offered all grades from Kindergarten to Secondary III (Grade 9),[13] plus some night classes for adults. Those wishing to complete high school had to go to Kuujjuaq. A few individuals pursued CEGEP (junior college) studies near Montreal. Kindergarten and Grades 1 and 2 were taught in Inuktitut, and the balance of the curriculum was in either English or French, with occasional classes in the native language.

Under the James Bay Agreement, Quaqtaq has a five-member health and social services committee. It advises the community on questions of hygiene and public health, while supervising the work of the local *inulirijiik* ('those who care about people'; the commmunity workers), two middle-aged women with basic training in how to deal with people suffering from family violence and other social problems. The village also has a committee against drug and alcohol abuse, and it sends a delegate to Nunavik's Kativik Council on Health and Social Services.

Four more locally run organizations, not related to the James Bay Agreement, may be found in Quaqtaq. Three of them are religious: the Anglican church council; the Women Helper Association (*Arnait ikajuqatigiit*), an Anglican self-help committee for women; and the Four Gospels Pentecostal church council. More will be said about them in the next chapter.

The fourth organization is the cooperative. Founded in 1973, and affiliated since 1981 with the Federation of Northern Quebec Cooperatives, it includes among its members almost all adult Quaqtamiut. The cooperative is administered by a six-person council, elected by the general assembly of members. In 1990 the mayor and school principal, who had also acted for a few years as president of the cooperative, was replaced in this function by a middle-aged hunter from Kindred A. The council appoints the cooperative manager, whose task is to serve the daily administration of the co-op store. In 1993 the manager was a man belonging to Kindred B, who had occupied this position since the late 1970s. The members send a delegate to the Federation of Northern Quebec Cooperatives, whose headquarters are situated near Montreal.

In addition to the local organizations, both levels of government, federal and provincial, maintain agencies in Quaqtaq. Nowadays, though, the federal government's only tangible presence in the village consists in the post office and in Telesat Canada's telephone and television antenna dish. By contrast, the government of Quebec still operates several organizations.

The nursing station, with its two transient nurses and local auxiliary personnel, receives patients with health problems. It looks after minor illnesses and dispatches more serious cases to hospitals in Kuujjuaq or Montreal. The nurses also visit the sick at home and supervise community hygiene and health.

Quebec's Department of Public Security is in charge of Quaqtaq's police station. In 1990 the policeman was a local man in his late twenties. He belonged to Sûreté du Québec (Quebec Provincial Police) and had completed a special training course for northern native constables. His duties consisted in maintaining law and order, and he had power to arrest offenders. In 1993, however, he resigned from his position, having found it too difficult to deal with delinquents who might be his friends or relatives. Police duties were then maintained by a Qallunaaq policeman from Kuujjuaq, who visited Quaqtaq a few days at a time, at irregular intervals.

Once or twice a year the village receives the visit of Nunavik's itinerant court of justice, with its Qallunaat judge, clerk, and appointed lawyers, and Inuit interpreters. For small crimes (e.g., public disorder, minor assault, or petty theft), offenders may be fined, sentenced to work for the community, or temporarily exiled to a neighbouring village. In 1993, for example, a young woman who had cheated the cooperative was sentenced to spend a month in Kuujjuaq. More major crimes generally entail a prison sentence served in a southern institution. The Quaqtaq police station has a cell, but it is only used for detaining offenders after their arrest.

Other provincial organizations include the Quebec housing authority (Société d'habitation du Québec), which owns the residences and supervises their maintenance;[14] Hydro-Québec, which operates Quaqtaq's power plant; and the Department of Transport, which manages and maintains the local airport and weather station.

Present-day Quaqtaq is thus endowed with a comprehensive set of economic, political, social, and educational organizations. These may sometimes enter in conflict with more traditional values and activities, but as we have begun to see in this chapter, Quaqtamiut seem quite able to reconcile their deepest identity with what the modern world has brought to their shores.

# 4

# Some Fundamentals of Identity

Identity in present-day Quaqtaq is anchored within several phenomena and institutions that play a crucial part in defining local culture. The phenomena that contribute to the uniqueness of Quaqtamiut include a privileged relationship with a territory rich in game, the small size of the community, a sense of shared family history, and a high degree of assertiveness towards the outside world.[1] Three elements, however, which will be dealt with in the following pages, stand out as particularly relevant to contemporary identity. These are kinship, religion, and language.

## Name and Kinship

### Names and Naming

When questioned about their identity, most Inuit – and the Quaqtamiut are no exception – generally answer in personal terms. Rather than mentioning that they belong to this or that ethnic group or local community, they prefer to stress that they bear specific names (*atiq*), inherited from other persons, and that these names define most of their relationships with the rest of the society.

As is well known, Inuit children receive names transmitted from other individuals, whether deceased or alive. The kinship and quasi-kinship relationships that used to link the former bearers of these personal appellations with bearers of other names are revived when the names are born again. For example, a man whose son is named after this man's mother[2] will call him *anaana* ('mother'), and the son will call his father *irniq* ('son'). Similarly, two persons bearing the names of deceased individuals who called themselves *aippaq* ('spouse') will use the same appellation when addressing each other. Those who share the same name call each other *sauniq* ('bone'). Naming is a serious topic. Whenever possible, an individual is addressed by a kinship term (e.g., 'mother,' 'spouse,' or 'little brother') rather than by one of his or her personal names. Formerly, it was considered impolite to ask somebody who he or she was.

In Quaqtaq children are usually given at least three names, although in many cases the total number of personal appellations may reach a total of seven or eight. These names generally belong to three categories:

1 The 'public' name. This is the name by which the child is known to those who do not have a special relationship (through kinship or as a *sauniq*) with him or her. It is typically used in the public sphere: at school, say, or on official documents. The name is generally chosen by the parents because they like it, and it includes 'modern' appellations (i.e., names never worn by the older generations) such as Norman, Laura, Troy, Jason, Sheila, Molly, or Dominique.[3]
2 The 'memorial' name(s). The child is also given the name(s) of the last deceased individual(s) within the community – or in another community if its family had a special link with that individual. He or she may also receive the name of one of his or her parents' most cherished relatives or friends, whether deceased or not.
3 The '*sauniq*' names. These are names of relatives or, more rarely, friends of the child's family, and they are generally transmitted within one particular kindred. The persons from whom the names originate may either be dead or alive. The names are ordinarily chosen by the parents or grandparents, but an individual may specifically request that such or such a name (including his or her own) be given to a newborn child;[4] this category is the most likely to include traditional (i.e., pre-Christian) names.[5]

In 1993, for example, a 2-year-old Quaqtaq girl was called Debbie ('public' appellation), Maasiu (a name given in memory of her recently deceased uncle), and Inugaluaq (the name of her *sauniq*, a female cousin of her mother). A newborn boy had received the names of Norman ('public'), Aqiggialuk ('memorial'), Saali, Miaji, Maasiu, Uili, Jaji, and Putulialuk (all *sauniit*).[6] Séguin (1991) mentions the case of a 10-year-old boy called Gary ('public' name), Alec and Sandy (*sauniik*; after, respectively, a deceased nephew of his mother and a Kuujjuaq man whose wife had requested the parents to give her husband's name to their child). The boy's younger sister was named Beatrice ('public'), Evie ('memorial,' after one of her mother's best friends, now deceased), and Ilisapi (*sauniq*, after her foster maternal grandmother).

According to the mother of these two children (as quoted by Séguin), the parents do not think that their child will have the same personality as his or her *sauniq*. But if he or she does, they will notice it. Formerly, the children whose biological sex differed from that of their *sauniq* (i.e., a boy named after a woman or a girl after a man) were often raised as if they were of the opposite gender. This custom, still prevalent in other parts of the Arctic (in Igloolik for instance; see Saladin d'Anglure 1992), has now disappeared from Quaqtaq. People also believed – and some still do – that a male child's sexual parts could split open a few moments after birth, his penis shrinking inside with the boy thus becoming a girl. This phenomenon was called *sipiniq* ('the splitting').

A few people bear a nickname (*atinnguaq* 'imitation of a name'), such as Miqquituq ('the one without hair') or Tautunngituq ('the blind one'). Many more have a qualifier (e.g., -*aluk* 'big', -*apik* 'small,' or -*kallak* 'short') attached to their principal name.

In addition to their personal names, all Quaqtamiut bear a family name (*atirusiq*, 'secondary name'). These were introduced by the federal government in the late 1950s, and they progressively replaced the so-called disc numbers[7] assigned at birth to all Inuit (on this topic, see Alia 1994). The bureaucrats in charge of giving surnames to the Inuit generally called each family after the main personal name of its oldest male member or of its most recently deceased male ancestor. For example, the offspring of Taqqiapik (he died in 1952) were surnamed Tukkiapik (the bureaucrats' spelling of their father's and grandfather's name). Later on, however, some individuals modified their family name, generally taking as new surname their own Inuit traditional name. For example, a young man named Peter Aupaluk Karesak (the last name being that of his deceased father) dropped his original surname to be simply known as Peter Aupaluk. His wife and children too bear the family name Aupaluk.

In Quaqtaq family names now seem to have become part of each person's identity. They are deemed useful for distinguishing between individuals who, because of the *sauniq* phenomenon, may bear the same first names. Transmitted within family groups, surnames also contribute to better identify the three kindreds, thus reinforcing these kindreds' existence. Children adopt the family name of their father (or maternal grandfather, if their mother is unwed), and married women that of their husband; therefore, kindreds increasingly tend to be identified as patrilateral units, that is, as groups of relatives descended from the same male ancestor, even if kinship remains bilateral.

Each kindred is characterized by the almost exclusive use of a few specific family names. In 1990 these were:

Kindred A: Tukkiapik, Okpik, Oovaut, Puttayuk, Nuvuuka, (Page),[8] (Savard), (Durocher)

Kindred B: Kulula, Pootoolik, Itigaituk, Kauki, Ningiuruvik, Aupaluk, (Deer), (Ilgun), (St Cyr)

Kindred C (including the CA and CB mixed families): Angnatuk, Oovaut, Kokkinerk, Jararusi, Papak.

Like family names, personal names also contribute to reinforce kindred identity. The *sauniq* names are generally transmitted within the boundaries of the family group. Kindreds, too, are family bound, and therefore many names are principally used by one kindred at the exclusion of the others.

On 1 January 1991 for example, ten out of thirteen Quaqtaq children born within Kindred A during the past six years (i.e., since 1 January 1985) had been given as principal *sauniq* the name of a person who belonged or had belonged to Kindred A; one had received its name from Kindred B, one from Kindred C, and one from an individual external to Quaqtaq. As concerns Kindred B, only half of the children (four out of eight) had their principal *sauniq* within their own kindred, but among the other half, three had received their name from outside Quaqtaq, and only one from Kindred A.

Within Kindred C, properly speaking, all five children born since 1985 were named for Kindred C individuals. However, four of the five children born in CA and CB mixed families had received their principal name from their mother's A or B kindred. The only exception was a child with a *sauniq* from Kindred C.

Up to a certain point, then, the *sauniq* system contributes to the reproduction of the kindreds from one generation to the other. The transmission of names helps to foster the identity of the kin groups, which have their own repertoires of *sauniq* and family names. On the other hand, the 'memorial' names, whose transmission transcends the kindreds' boundaries, reconstruct, so to speak, the entire community, by continually renaming all of its newborn children with the appellations formerly worn by its deceased members. In this way, the naming patterns contribute to support, at the same time, the personal, family, and collective identities of Quaqtamiut.

*Kinship*

Family and kindred identity are also supported by kinship (*ilagiinniq*) relations. As a result of intermarriage among the Tuvaaluk people during the 1950s, and, more recently, between Quaqtamiut and children of Killiniq immigrants, each Quaqtaq household is linked to at least one other household by kinship ties. This means that in every family, the father and/or mother, together with their children, are related by blood, adoption, or marriage to at least one parent, brother, sister, cousin, adopted relative, or in-law, who is also a Quaqtamiuq. In most cases the families have several relatives in the village.

For the great majority of households, the nearest relative is a primary one, that is, an individual with whom one is linked through a parent–child or sibling–sibling relation. Out of a total of fifty households residing in Quaqtaq on 1 January 1991 forty-five had at least one married primary relative who also lived in the village, within another household (see Figure 1). Three more households had secondary – but no primary – relatives. Two of them were headed by widows whose closest kin relationships were their deceased husband's brothers and/or sisters. The third consisted of only one individual, a young bachelor whose parents had died several years before, and who only had two aunts (and many cousins) in the village. A fourth unit was headed by a woman whose closest relative was a first cousin, and a last one comprised a man, orphaned as a child, who had been sheltered, but never adopted, by his mother's cousin. This man's wife was from outside Quaqtaq, and therefore his only local relatives were this now-deceased cousin's widow and children.

A word on adoption is in order here. Like all other Inuit, Quaqtamiut adopt children – or give them into adoption – quite frequently. Older people, for example, regularly adopt babies, often their own grandchildren, because, they say, they need youngsters to enliven the house and help them with domestic tasks. On 1 January 1991, of the 219 Inuit of all ages then residing in Quaqtaq 70 had been adopted at birth or shortly after. A full 32 per cent of all Quaqtamiut had thus gone through adoption.[9] For Inuit adopted children have the same family status as biological offspring, and therefore, when assessing kinship relations no distinction is made here between them and the non-adopted children.

All Quaqtaq families form a continuous web of kin and relatives (Figure 1). No member of the community is completely isolated, that is, without ties to at least one other member, who has himself or herself a sibling, parent, or cousin in another household, which is itself linked to another family, and so on. This does not mean, however, that everybody is related to everybody else. Because over the past decades there have practically been no marriages between members of Kindreds A and B,[10] and because the former Killinirmiut (Kindred C) are only beginning to wed the offspring of older families, kinship relationships within any kindred are much more frequent and close-knit than those linking kindreds with each other. Within a kindred, the households are typically linked through parent–child and/or sibling–sibling relations. The ties between Kindred C and the two others, however, involve a son-in-law (belonging to Kindred C) and his wife's parents. Between Kindreds A and B the kinship relationships are more distant, involving cousins rather than brothers and sisters.

Quaqtaq's three kindreds are thus principally composed of primary relatives, who, as shall be seen, maintain privileged relationships among themselves. Two of these kindreds are a direct continuation of the local groups that occupied Tuvaaluk's winter camps over fifty years ago. In January 1943, for example, the families of (husband/wife) Taqqiapik/Taqaq, Inuluk/Arjangajuk, and Jaiku/Lali, ancestors to most members of Kindred A, were living in Quaqtaq, while those of Nua Masik/Iiva, Matiusi Kululaaq/Aani Anautaq, Tajara (a widow), and Nunalik/Niqiguluk, the forebears of Kindred B, spent the cold season in Iggiajaq.[11] These camp groups had themselves taken the place of the local bands that used to travel across the Tuvaaluk and western Ungava areas before the establishment of the trading posts. The presence of kindreds in contemporary Quaqtaq – as in other Inuit communities – thus perpetuates a form of social organization – one based on kinship – that predates the present era and has most probably always characterized the Inuit people.[12]

Until the last wave of sedentarization and economic modernization, in the 1960s, most activities were based on kinship relations. As seen in Chapter 2, the trapping teams, Peterhead crews, and smaller camp groups observed in Tuvaaluk in the 1940s and 1950s were almost exclusively composed of close relatives, as were the nomadic bands and *umiatuinnaq* (skin boat) crews that preceded them. When questioned about their preferences in terms of hunting partners, most men answered that they felt much more secure and at ease when going out on the land with primary relatives.[13]

Nowadays, kinship has ceased to play any significant economic role in Quaqtaq. However, it preserves some of its importance as a factor for understanding residential patterns. Migration to and from the village is motivated in large part by the desire to join relatives. At a more fundamental level, most households are still based on a parent–child relation. Out of fifty households established in Quaqtaq on 1 January 1991, twenty-four comprised a complete nuclear family (two parents with their unmarried offspring and, occasionally, their daughter's young children), thirteen a one-parent nuclear family (usually a widow – or, much more rarely, a single or divorced woman – and her children), and thirteen more a single individual living alone or with a girl- or boyfriend. Wherever possible parents and their married offspring preferred to occupy neighbouring houses.

Kinship also constitutes a favourite locale for day-to-day social relations. In 1990, for example, a sample of eighteen Quaqtamiut were questioned about their best friends (*piqati* 'one with whom one does something').[14] Thirty-one of the friends mentioned were relatives of the respondents, and twenty-nine of these belonged to the respondent's kindred. In several cases the informants mentioned primary relatives (their own parents, children, or siblings) as being their best friends. Almost all of a respondent's friends were of the same gender and age group as he or she was. Only nine *piqatiit* had no kinship relation with the informant.

Proportions were similar in the case of the individuals most often visited by the respondents. These were generally the same as the best friends and, on average, visits occurred three times a week. As far as mutual help was concerned, a majority of people asserted that they endeavoured to help anybody in need, rather than just their own relatives. In reality, however, sharing and helping mainly occurred within the families and kindreds.

Several Quaqtamiut state that kinship relationships are not as important now as they used to be. They often mention that parents and children do not understand each other any more. They also speak of the alleged instability of many young couples – who, they assert, are prone to part on the slightest pretext – or the small knowledge the children have of traditional kinship terminology. Many youngsters, for instance, now call their mother 'mom,' rather than *anaana*, the proper kinship term. Blame for all this is laid on sedentarization, television, or the attitude of the parents, who, according to some informants, would not teach their offspring the difference between good and bad habits.

As seen from outside, though, the situation appears better than it looks to these critics. Kinship relationships may be undergoing some stress, but the family still preserves its importance in Quaqtaq. It is true that each age group possesses its own culture: children do not have the same interests as adolescents or young adults, and middle-aged individuals behave differently from the elderly. The respective interests of men and women may also be considered as somewhat divergent. Within the household, however, relationships are generally harmonious, even if problems arise from time to time. The different generations communicate with each other, and many Quaqtamiut –

those involved in the school, for example – make genuine efforts to integrate the youngsters within the community and transmit to them the local culture. Despite some marital instability, divorce remains infrequent, and babies are generally welcome.[15] In a small place like Quaqtaq, where everyone knows everybody else, and where contact with unspoilt nature is permanent, problems occur less acutely than in larger settlements.

This does not mean, however, that social and personal difficulties are non-existent. Between 1989 and 1993 Quaqtaq witnessed four violent deaths, including the suicide of three young women. Some of these problems are linked to alcohol and drug abuse, which, in turn, may be the result of boredom and the lack of opportunities for the young. Caught between life on the land, about which they do not know enough, and the modern labour market, whose doors seem reluctant to open up to them, many young people have developed a feeling of being totally useless. This perceived uselessness shows up in interviews. When asked if the young have something to teach their elders, Quaqtamiut of all ages answer negatively or mention trivialities (e.g., the old can learn a few English words from the young). According to psychologist Dominique Collin (1991), such a perception is compounded by the fact that youngsters have now developed a 'modern' identity, widely open to the outside world, which cannot find its place in a still predominantly social-symbolic universe of the 'premodern' type, one that limits itself to rather narrow local concerns.

Despite such occasional clashes between modernity and tradition, the community functions rather smoothly, even if a few of its members do not try – or do not wish – to integrate with the others. These marginals are Quaqtaq's transient – and some of its resident – Qallunaat.

Any Qallunaaq living in Quaqtaq for at least five years is considered a full-fledged member of the community,[16] and those who marry a local Inuk become beneficiaries of the James Bay Agreement. Quaqtamiut do not oppose the presence of these people who are 'seized by their spouse' (*aippaminut tigujaujut*), that is, who join sides with the Inuit, stating that such individuals may be useful to the community. This attitude probably stems from a long tradition, whereby the traders and weather station operators stationed in Tuvaaluk used to take a local wife during their stay. It seems, however, that many Qallunaat, whether resident or transient, hesitate to socialize with the local people. They never visit Inuit homes, they do not mix with Inuit outside the workplace, and, needless to say, no Qallunaaq speaks Inuktitut.

Such an attitude, which to a great extent is the result of major social and cultural differences, is generally resented by Quaqtamiut. They perceive some Qallunaat as haughty individuals, who want to be thought of as models to follow rather than as *inuuqatiit* ('companions who live the same life'). Alternately, Qallunaat may be seen as competitors, who steal jobs that should belong to the Inuit.

This perception is echoed in the talk of a number of local Qallunaat, who assert that Inuit will never be able to replace them completely, or who boast that they were successful getting this or that job which, until then, had been occupied by an Inuk. Such words, however, are by no means characteristic of all of Quaqtaq's Qallunaat. Some individuals, more numerous among the residents than among the transients, have become well-respected members of the community.[17]

Qallunaat are rarely included within the system of kinship relations, except jokingly. A parent-in-law may call his or her daughter's non-Inuk husband *ningauk* ('son-in-law'), but the use of kinship terminology when addressing a Qallunaaq – or speaking about him or her – does not usually extend beyond such immediate relations. By excluding a whole category of individuals from one's own network of relatives, kinship thus contributes to delimit the two ethnic components of Quaqtaq society, in the same way it helps to preserve kindreds within the village. Its bearing on identity thus becomes obvious. At the community level, kinship reinforces the Inuit identity of all native Quaqtamiut (a non-Inuk cannot be a kin), but simultaneously it operates primarily within subgroupings that reproduce pre-community patterns deeply ingrained within the local cultural identity.

## Religion

These patterns show up in the religious affiliation of Quaqtamiut. On 1 July 1990 the Inuit residents of Quaqtaq belonged to two different creeds. A little more than half (111 individuals[18]) were Anglicans, the balance (101 persons) being affiliated with the Four Gospels Pentecostal (also known as Christian Fellowship) Church. Four individuals had been baptized Catholics. Three of them attended the Anglican church, while the fourth preferred to associate with the Pentecostals. Among the non-Inuit residents, four were nominal Catholics, one was a practising Pentecostal, and the sixth (born in Turkey) belonged to the Moslem faith. Of the Anglicans 72 per cent (80/111) belonged to Kindred A, 5 per cent (6/111) to Kindred B, and 23 per cent (25/111) to Kindred C. By contrast, the largest portion of the Pentecostal Inuit (48/101, or 48 per cent) were members of Kindred B; only 20 per cent of them belonged to Kindred A, and 33 per cent to Kindred C.

In other words, 80 per cent of the members of Kindred A were Anglicans, and 20 per cent were affiliated with the Pentecostal church. Conversely, the vast majority (89 per cent) of the members of Kindred B were Pentecostals, and only six individuals (11 per cent) were Anglicans. For all these people, then, kindred and religious affiliation were almost synonymous.[19] Within Kindred C, however, religious loyalties were more evenly distributed; 43 per cent of the kindred's members (25/58) were Anglicans and 57 per cent Pentecostals.

## Religious Sentiment

Religious sentiment is generally high among Quaqtamiut, whatever their affiliation. Apart from church attendance, which on an average Sunday involves only a minority of the population, it expresses itself through frequent recourse to prayer (*tutsianiq*), whether individually or in family, and through a quasi-general respect for the Third Commandment, which forbids work (including hunting and fishing) on Sunday (*allituqalirtilugu* 'when they abide by a taboo').

Most Quaqtamiut strongly believe in God (*Guuti*), incarnated in His Son Jesus Christ (*Jisusi Kraistusi*). They also believe in the existence of spirits, good and evil. The good spirits are the angels (*anirnisiat*, 'good breaths,' or *ingillit*), and the bad ones (the devils, headed by *Satanasi*, Satan), are generally equated to the *tuurngait*, the auxiliary spirits of the traditional shaman (*angakkuq*). Some people, however, assert that the *tuurngait* are not necessarily bad, because they often helped the shaman to accomplish good deeds (e.g., healing the sick or bringing the game back).

People are sometimes possessed by evil spirits: devils, *uirsait* (invisible husbands) or *nuliarsait* (invisible wives). Exorcism may be necessary to get rid of them (see Kirmayer et al. 1994).

Besides their visible body (*timi*), all human beings have three invisible components: the breath, the name(s), and the soul. The breath (*anirniq*) gives life to the body. When it stops the body dies and starts to decay. The name (*atiq*) is transmitted to newborn infants, thus being revived in the youngest members of the community. The third component, the soul (*tarniq*), is immortal. When the body dies, the soul either goes to heaven (*qilak* 'the sky') or hell (*kappianartuvik* 'the big fearful place'), according to the person's deeds during his or her life. The soul interacts with the body through intelligence (*sila*), which enables the individual to make a choice between the good (*piujuq*) and the evil (*piunngituq*). This choice becomes possible when one has developed enough thought (*isuma*) to be able to act reasonably. The word *sila* also means 'outside,' 'weather,' 'universe' (*silar-juaq* 'the huge *sila*'), among other things. This shows that, for Inuit, intelligence is perceived as a kind of microcosm containing the whole world. The individual is thus indissociably linked to his or her environment.

From the first decades of the twentieth century Quaqtamiut have become genuine Christians. Shamans have completely disappeared, and the old myths and rituals are no longer known or practised.[20] For most people faith (*uppiniq* 'the act of believing') in God, Jesus, the soul, and Christian teachings in general is essential. It shows how one should behave in order not to let the evil forces dominate the world. Some assert that the only important truth (*sulijuq* 'what corresponds to reality'), as taught by faith, is that earth will pass, but heaven will stand. One should thus live a good life in order to remain on heaven's side.

Several Christian virtues are in direct continuity with some of the most important traditional values. Quaqtamiut consider mutual aid to be a fundamental characteristic of their Inuit identity. An *inutuinnaq* ('genuine Inuk') is generous towards others, helps them before they even ask, and refrains from cheating them. He or she is also thankful, readily expressing his or her gratitude (*nakursaniq*) to those who show him or her kindness. Most people, then, do not see any contradiction between past and present attitudes because both traditional custom and Christian teachings encourage mutual aid, honesty, and gratitude. When praying, for example, Quaqtamiut are often inspired by gratitude or by their duties towards their kin. At the end of the day, hunters and fishers frequently thank God for their catch. One hunter told me that once, when about to drown (his snowmobile had broken through sea ice), he thought about his responsibilities towards his children and prayed to be saved. He then found the strength to wade ashore and return home.

In view of these similarities between past and present, the passage from shamanism to Christianity should not be seen as a total break between two antagonistic world-views,[21] but rather as a partial transformation of the Inuit patterns of communication with the suprahuman. From the 1920s to the 1940s Nunavik witnessed the advent of syncretic religious movements, all of them short-lived, that mixed traditional and Christian beliefs and practices, thus setting up a kind of aboriginal Christianity at a moment when shamans were being replaced by catechists (*tutsiatitsijiit* 'those who make people pray').[22] Conversely, one of the last *angakkuit*, Pilurtuuti, tried to integrate Christian elements within shamanism, by enlisting the help of a biblical lion as one of his auxiliary spirits (Saladin d'Anglure 1984).

The shamans finally went into oblivion, but several of their functions (e.g., supervising collective rituals, praying for the sick, and advising people) were taken on by the catechists. Many traditional beliefs endured under Christianity, and some of them still constitute an integral part of the world-view of modern Quaqtamiut. For example, the three invisible components (*anirniq, atiq,* and *tarniq*) of human individuality are essentially the same as the three souls of the pre-Christian Inuit (see Chapter 1). The main difference lies in the fact that, formerly, the fate of the *tarniq* in the next world was linked to the type of death the individual had suffered. If death had been violent (e.g., by accident or murder), the *tarniq* went to a pleasanter place than if one had died from illness or old age. Nowadays, the fate of the *tarniq* is in accordance with the life (good or bad) the individual has lived.

Attitudes towards animals, generally imbued with respect, have not changed much since older times. To give one example, when a freshly killed seal is brought into the house, a few drops of fresh water are still often poured into its mouth because the animal is thought to be thirsty. Some people believe that the seal's soul is so pleased by the respect it is shown that when reborn it will allow itself to be caught again by the same hunter.

The belief in *tuurngait* (spirits) is still prevalent, and some individuals (*ilisiittut* 'sorcerers') are said to know how to enlist the spirits' help to cast evil spells over their neighbours. Two alleged female *ilisiittut*, both of them now deceased, lived in Quaqtaq during the past decades. One also occasionally hears about ghosts (*ijuruit* or *angirraniit*) and other supranatural beings, such as *inugagulligait* (goblins), *amautilialuk* ('the big one with a baby-carrying pouch,' an ogre), and *lumaajuq* (the mythical mother of narwhals).[23] Nowadays, though, very few people appear to believe in – or care about – the existence of such creatures. This is not because of the 'heathen' contents of these beliefs; it is simply because goblins or ogres do not have any meaningful part to play in modern life.

In spite of modernity, contact with the other world remains easy for Quaqtamiut. Some individuals, for example, can predict how they will die. The mother of a resident said that she would pass away without knowing about it, and she departed in her sleep, whereas his father had predicted that he would not die at home, and he died accidentally near Quaqtaq. One young man recounts how, when a child, he once died after having knocked his head. He wanted to enter Heaven, but felt pulled back and was revived. After having fainted during a hospital stay, an older woman saw a Qallunaaq who was standing erect in front of her.[24] Because she did not want to die, she prayed and then regained consciousness.

*The Anglicans*

Apart from such individual occurrences, religious sentiment also expresses itself collectively in the two established religions in Quaqtaq. Of these, the Anglican is the oldest and has the most adherents, with 52 per cent of the local Inuit population.

The Anglicans were the first Christian missionaries (*ajuqirtuijiit* 'those who empower through teaching') to evangelize Nunavik.[25] Present at Fort George (Chisasibi) on James Bay, as early as the 1850s, they moved to southeastern Hudson Bay in 1876, when the Reverend Edmund J. Peck (Uqarmak 'the wonderful speaker') established the first mission among the Quebec Inuit, at Little Whale River. Later on, in 1899, another mission was opened near the Fort Chimo (Kuujjuaq) HBC store. As seen in Chapter 1, the northern Nunavik people, including the Tuvaalummiut, were first exposed to Christian teachings when they visited the trading post, but quite early some Inuit took the responsibility of acting as catechists, bringing the Word of God to those who were unable or unwilling to travel to Kuujjuaq. They also brought literacy, teaching to their family and friends the syllabic characters introduced by the Anglicans. These characters enabled the Inuit to read the Bible and prayer books, as well as to write in their own language.

By the early 1930s all Nunavimmiut had been baptized in the Anglican church. There were Qallunaat missionaries in Kuujjuaq, Kuujjuaraapik (Great Whale River), and Inukjuak (on Hudson Bay), and Inuit catechists (lay readers) in most local camps. In 1936 the Roman Catholics, already present in other parts of the Canadian Arctic, decided to establish their own missions in northern Quebec (Dorais and Saladin d'Anglure 1988). After Kangiqsujuaq (1936) and Ivujivik (1938), the Oblate Fathers (*itsirarjuat* 'the huge ones who bend forward while turning their back to people'[26]) opened residences in Kuujjuaraapik (1946), Quaqtaq (1947), and a few other locations. At their peak, in the late 1950s and early 1960s, seven Catholic missions were to be found in Nunavik, each of them hosting one or two resident missionaries.

Nunavimmiut did not feel the need to become Catholics because they were already Christian. Only a few families and individuals, living principally around Kangiqsujuaq, converted to the new denomination. Some of them later moved to Tuvaaluk, and two or three conversions occurred locally, but the total number of Catholics residing in Quaqtaq never exceeded twenty individuals. The Quaqtaq mission closed in 1967 (see Chapter 2), and the four remaining Catholics started worshipping at the

Anglican church,[27] although they continued being visited from time to time by the Kangiqsujuaq priest, who was soon to become the last resident Catholic missionary in Nunavik. For a few years, then, Anglicanism was the only religion practised in the village.

For Anglicans faith and prayer are very important, although religious activities seem to be perceived as individual, rather than collective affairs. Sunday services are generally attended by a very small number of worshippers, most of them aged, because people prefer to pray at home. Many assert that they try to involve their children in churchgoing, but, according to them, the young are not interested in organized religion. An Anglican Sunday school operates sporadically, and faith is taught at school, but most youngsters do not continue open religious practice.

The current Anglican church building, erected in the 1980s thanks to voluntary labour, stands on the west side of the village. It includes a porch, a tiny vestry, and the main church hall. This last contains about a dozen benches – divided into two sections by a central aisle – and a small altar and pulpit in front. Men and women usually sit on opposite sides of the aisle, although this custom is not respected as strictly as it used to be. Ornamentation is very simple. It mainly consists in a cross, some sealskin appliqués on the altar-cloth, and a few inscriptions in syllabic characters (such as *Guuti qujattauli* 'May God be thanked!') on the walls.

In 1990 the principal lay reader (catechist) was a man in his mid-fifties, assisted by two older individuals, a man and a woman. The men belonged to Kindred A, and the woman was one of the very few members of Kindred B to practise Anglicanism. The three of them, wearing a surplice, conducted the Sunday morning service.

A typical service lasts for about an hour and fifteen minutes and consists in prayers, readings from the Bible, a few hymns, and a sermon delivered by the principal catechist. The Holy Eucharist is only celebrated on the rare occasions that an ordained minister visits Quaqtaq. The entire service is conducted in Inuktitut, and sermons often include allusions to the local context, such as, 'Jesus is serious when he says that the Kingdom of God is coming, even if he does not know when it will happen (only his father knows); it is like the Inuit of old, who said that the caribou would come back, even if it seemed as if this animal had disappeared forever; and look, the caribou is now back.'[28]

Although they nominally depend on the Kuujjuaq minister and, ultimately, on the Bishop of the Arctic, who resides in Iqaluit (Baffin Island), the local Anglican catechists, as well as the elected church council, are quite free to organize things as they see fit. Since the 1970s, however, they have had to face a big challenge: the increasing growth of the Pentecostal faith in Quaqtaq and the rest of the Arctic. They reacted to this challenge by consolidating religious education and developing social action. For example, several Anglican women now belong to the Women Helper Association (*Arnait ikajuqatigiit*), an informal group whose task is to support those in material or spiritual need.

## The Pentecostals

Despite such initiatives, Pentecostalism did not cease making gains in Quaqtaq. Introduced in the Canadian Arctic by Qallunaat preachers during the late 1960s, it entered Nunavik around 1970, where it immediately met with success. In 1978 a group of Quaqtamiut who had been in contact with Kangirsuk Pentecostals established a congregation in the village. They built a small prayer house (the Four Gospels Church) where they met once or twice a week. In 1981 the congregation already comprised forty-three members (27 per cent of the population), who all belonged to Kindred B. Nine years later this figure had more than doubled: 102 Pentecostals (101 Inuit and one resident non-Inuk) were to be found in Quaqtaq.[29] They accounted for 48 per cent of all native residents.

It was mentioned in Chapter 2 that the religious independence of the members of Kindred B, who left Anglicanism to become Pentecostals, probably occurred because, during the late 1970s and early 1980s, they only played a minor role within Quaqtaq's administrative bodies. For them, the new creed might have symbolically compensated for their minority status. This could also explain why more than half of the households belonging to Kindred C have now joined the Pentecostals.[30] It should be added too that since the 1950s, all Anglican catechists have been members of Kindred A, thus leaving the other groups of families out of the socio-religious power structure.

This is not the entire explanation, however. Pentecostalism holds its own appeal, whose importance should not be neglected. The new creed is perceived by its followers as a personal relation with Jesus rather than as a corpus of doctrine, like Anglicanism or Catholicism. The adherents assert that the Pentecostal teachings are easy to understand, and that they enable people to believe by themselves. As expressed by a member of the Four Gospels Church, the Pentecostals have *maligait* ('directions to be followed'), rather than *piqujait* ('commands'). In other words, Pentecostalism shows people how to relate to God, without compelling them to blindly obey the preacher's injunctions.

A proper relation with God brings changes to one's own life. Many Pentecostals stress that religion helped them overcome their alcohol and drug problems. A statement like the following is typical: 'I was Anglican. I had faith, but I heard about this new creed and I decided that I wanted to serve Jesus. I understood that I should give up alcohol, cards, and bingo. I wanted to be good and the new creed showed me how to behave in order to improve myself.'[31]

The Holy Bible is considered the basis (*tunngavik*) of all teachings. It is by strictly adhering to its precepts that one may change his or her life. The Bible is like a guide showing what to do to serve Jesus. This explains why the Pentecostals consider religious education to be fundamental. The Four Gospels Church runs a regular Sunday school, and several parents discuss the Bible with their children. Some complain, however, that older children are not really interested in learning about religion.

Going to church is considered to be important, even if on an average Sunday, only about twenty to thirty people participate in the morning service.[32] The present prayer house is a rather large structure, built in the late 1980s on the east side of the village. It stands adjacent to the original church, which now serves as Sunday school. Ornamentation is almost non-existent. A few religious posters and two inscriptions – one in Inuktitut and one in English – adorn the walls.

The Sunday morning service lasts for about an hour. It mainly comprises readings, hymns, and preaching, but it also happens that a member of the congregation comes to the front of the church to bear testimony on, for example, his or her encounters with God, moral weaknesses, or personal feelings. The atmosphere may then become filled with emotion, some people weeping, others shouting 'Alleluia,' and the preacher trying to comfort the testimony bearer.

In 1990 the Quaqtaq preacher was a middle-aged hunter, a core member of Kindred B, involved for many years in the Four Gospels congregation.[33] Three other individuals, a man and two women also belonging to Kindred B, were in charge of music. The hymns – in Inuktitut or, more rarely, English – are accompanied by percussion instruments and a pump organ, or sung by a solo voice. Many are in a rhythmical mood. Some hymns appear to have originally been written in a Northwest Territories dialect, but several were composed by a local young man, whose musical reputation reaches well beyond Quaqtaq. They relate his spiritual experience when he 'falls' (*katatsuni*), struck by the Holy Ghost.

Elements such as these (music with a beat; hymns sung in English) certainly give Pentecostalism a touch of modernity that is not found in Anglicanism or Catholicism. This modernity also expresses itself in other small ways. During services, for instance, people may remit their monetary offerings in envelopes identified by their name, in order to facilitate the issue of receipts for income tax purposes.[34] Besides Inuktitut prayer books, English and French Bibles are also available to Qallunaat visitors.

Quaqtaq's Four Gospels Church plays a leading role within Canadian Inuit Pentecostalism. In March 1990 it organized a Bible convention in the village. The meetings were attended by several Nunavik and Baffin Region Inuit, as well as by a few Qallunaat from southern Canada and the United States. Preaching was in English and Inuktitut, with consecutive interpretation in the other language. As a token of modernity, the whole proceedings were recorded on video, to be later broadcast on northern television.

Pentecostal modernity also shows off in some typical attitudes towards work and money. Most believers insist on the importance of working steadily and regularly, and they often point out that every service rendered should receive its due monetary reward, except, of course, if it is done for charity.[35] Formal education is highly valued too, as a means to acquire professional skills. This may partly explain why, in 1990, the principal, the secretary, and six out of the seven Inuit teachers at the Quaqtaq school were Pentecostals.

At the same time as it is modern, Pentecostalism revives some very traditional Inuit religious attitudes. Like shamanism, it is based on a personal relation with the supranatural rather than on a corpus of doctrine, with the difference that Pentecostalism relies on a written guide, the Bible, to explain how to properly establish this relation. The similarity between both traditions is implicitly acknowledged by the Quaqtaq Pentecostals, when they assert that the shamans of old established relationships with the evil spirits (*tuurngait*), whereas they themselves prefer to turn away from the devils, to relate to Jesus and his angels.

Some aspects of Pentecostal religious expression also remind one of shamanism. These include the public confession of one's own weaknesses or the inspiration found in contacts with the Holy Ghost. Such modern reevaluation and reutilization of traditional attitudes and practices probably account for the appeal of Pentecostalism, which, according to its followers, is becoming increasingly visible (*nuitavalliajuq*) in the North.

On the whole, then, religion contributes much to the identity of Quaqtamiut. At the surface level, the divisions between Anglicans and Pentecostals, which roughly correspond to the kindred boundaries, reinforce the presence of family groups within the community. These divisions, however, should not be exaggerated. The members of the two religions do not fight each other, even if, on the occasion of municipal elections, they may struggle to elect an Anglican or Pentecostal mayor. Everybody is genuinely interested in furthering Quaqtaq's interests, independently of his or her religious affiliation. People are, however, concerned with the diminishing importance of religious practice among the young generations. In the words of an Anglican elder, it is as if religion were on the edge of a table from which it could fall at any time.

For many Quaqtamiut, religion is a mode of social identity, a locus where people can get together in the security of a well-known system of beliefs, practices, and attitudes. It is also a domain that, despite the exogenous origin of Christianity is almost totally controlled by the Inuit. The Four Gospels Church, although loosely related to the Confederation of Christian Fellowship Churches, is completely independent from any external authority, and the Anglicans also enjoy an almost total freedom of action. Hence the tremendous importance of religion in terms of self-identification. Religion appears even more significant, if we consider that the sentiment of communion with the supranatural it carries on has not faltered since pre-Christian times. Remarkably visible in Pentecostalism, where traditional attitudes are reinterpreted in an extremely modern way, this continuity between the old and the new is also very much present within Anglicanism.

## Language

Besides kinship and religion, language is one of the most fundamental elements of Quaqtaq's identity. In many ways, Inuktitut appears as the dominant language of the community. It constitutes the usual means of communication of all Inuit residents, and many of them do not understand any other language. Two other speech forms, however, English and French, are also in daily use in the village. The predominance of Inuktitut is thus being challenged by the presence of the Qallunaat tongues. This is why it is important to cast a look at the linguistic behaviour of Quaqtamiut, as well as at their opinions on language and identity.

### Language Use

To the casual visitor, everyday life in Quaqtaq appears to be almost totally conducted in Inuktitut. This is the language most often heard on the street, in the stores, at church, or in the town hall, as well as in all Inuit homes, including those headed by a mixed couple. A majority of the local written messages and radio programs are in Inuktitut too. In fact, the only really multilingual environment is to be found at school, where most of the teaching is conducted in English or French, and where pupils are requested to speak their second language at all times, except, of course, during classes dealing with Inuit language and culture.

Beyond this façade, however, the linguistic situation is a little more complex. According to the Canadian census, for example, only 65 of all 235 residents and transients living in Quaqtaq on 1 June 1991 were monolingual in Inuktitut. This means that 70.5 per cent of the 220 Inuit residents were bilingual or, in a few cases, trilingual. The fifteen non-Inuit residents and transients were generally bilingual in French and English (one was bilingual in Turkish and English). None spoke Inuktitut, although one resident, who had been living in the community since the early 1970s, understood it quite well. The most widespread non-native language was English (*qallunaatitut* 'the language of the Qallunaat'), spoken as a third, second, or first language by a total of 155 Quaqtamiut. Thirty-five of these people were also fluent in French (*uiguititut* 'the language of the Oui-oui'), but only fifteen individuals spoke French without any knowledge of English.

This does not mean that the Quaqtaq Inuit were losing their language. Inuktitut was the mother tongue of all native Quaqtamiut, and the only language understood by most preschool children. In 1991 (according to census data), 220 individuals stated that the principal or unique language they used at home was Inuktitut, whereas only fifteen persons, all of them presumably Qallunaat, declared it was French or English.

At closer glance, though, language use appears more finely shaded than what can be inferred from statistics. For example, although all eighteen respondents included in my 1990 sample state that they speak Inuktitut fluently, only six of them, schooled in English up to the secondary or post-secondary level, declare that they are also fluent in the Qallunaat language. Five more individuals, including two older men[36] and three younger persons, say that they can hold a conversation in English, without considering themselves to be completely fluent in this language. Another five individuals, four middle-aged and elderly women, and an adolescent whose principal school language is French, state that they understand some English without really speaking the language. Only two old persons admit to a total lack of knowledge of the Qallunaat tongue.

As for French, it is totally unknown by most (eleven of eighteen) of my informants. Six persons, however, two elderly individuals (a man and a woman) and four younger ones, declare that they understand some French, and only one respondent, an adolescent schooled in the Oui-oui tongue, is able to hold a conversation in this language.

The older bilingual informants make exclusive use of Inuktitut when speaking to other Inuit. They – and a few monolingual individuals – assert that some children may try to address them in English, but that they always answer in the native language.

Among the younger adults, schooled in the Qallunaat tongue, the situation is somewhat different. All of them mix their Inuktitut speech with English words and sentences when speaking to their peers. Some specify that they turn to English when no Inuktitut word is available, or when the available word or expression is too long. For example, many prefer to say 'next week' rather than *pinasuarusiulaartumi* or 'see you' in place of *takuniarpuguk*. When discussing more technical matters (e.g., politics or administration), those fluent in English often prefer to use this language. A few occasionally address their children in English, in order, so they say, to train them in their second language.

Many children use English – or French – expressions in their speech, but Inuktitut remains their primary means of communication. In the bi-ethnic families, the youngsters usually speak French or English to their father, and Inuktitut to their mother and siblings. A few of them, though, may answer their father in Inuktitut, or occasionally address their mother in English or French. As for the parents, they communicate with each other in English.

At the workplace everybody speaks Inuktitut all the time, unless he or she must address a Qallunaaq. Written communications, however, are almost exclusively in English, except when directed towards the local population. Even documents emanating from, or sent to, the headquarters of Inuit organizations are generally written up in English. The municipal council deliberates in Inuktitut, but the minutes of its proceedings are bilingual.

With one exception (a man who became blind in his youth), all Quaqtaq Inuit over 7 years of age, whether schooled or not, are able to read and write Inuktitut in syllabic characters. Among my sample of 1990, thirteen respondents declare that they write syllabics fluently, and four more state that they write it with some difficulty. Three of these are young men schooled entirely in English (two of whom write this language without any problems), and the fourth is an older man who admits that because he does not write very often, he tends to forget some symbols. The older informants learned syllabics by themselves, often with the help of a parent or older sibling, whereas the youngest were taught this script at school.

The few Quaqtamiut who became bilingual without being really schooled are able to read English, but they feel more comfortable in Inuktitut. For people with a little more formal education – typically those having completed elementary school – Inuktitut is easier to write, but they read better in English. Among the younger people, some also read French quite fluently. As for those Inuit who have completed high school or beyond, they find it easier to read and write English (if they were only taught in this language), or do not have problems in either their first or second language, if they had some Inuktitut at school.

A study showed that the written Inuktitut of the Quaqtaq schoolchildren is particularly good, as is their written English (Stairs 1990). They are able to build grammatically correct sentences in both languages, although in Inuktitut these sentences appear to older speakers as shorter and simpler than what is usually found in the traditional speech. An example of this difference could be as follows. Whereas a more traditional Inuk would say (and write): *Silaqqitualuutillugu, tupatsimatsunilu nirigiirsunilu aullasivuq* ('While the weather is very nice, being awake and after having finished to eat, he starts to leave'), a school-aged Quaqtamiuq would have: *Silaqqitualuk. Tupattulu, nirijurlu, ammalu aullasivuq* ('The weather is very nice. He wakes up and eats, and also starts to leave'). Both sentences are grammatically correct, but the second displays a simpler and more direct style than the first. According to Stairs's study, the good performance of the children could be a reflection of the competence of their teachers, as well as that Inuktitut is still predominant in their community.

It remains to be seen, however, to what extent these children are actually interested in writing and reading Inuit texts. Most young and middle-aged adults schooled in English, including some Inuktitut teachers, admit that it is easier for them to read English, and that, given the choice, they prefer written materials published in this language. They stress that what is available in Inuktitut – mostly school, religious, and technical literature – is often uninteresting and clumsily written. Several subscribe to anglophone magazines (e.g., *Time*, *Reader's Digest*, or religious periodicals), but others declare that they do not read much, except, perhaps, comic books, which are ubiquitous in Inuit homes. A majority of the bilingual Quaqtamiut declare that they occasionally read texts in Inuktitut, such as the literature published by various aboriginal organizations. Most monolingual individuals also read these.

In addition to printed media, the Quaqtaq people also have access to television and radio. Satellite television has been available since 1983, when the Nunavik authorities lifted the ban they had originally put on this medium of communication. In June 1990 Quaqtamiut could watch three channels: CBC North (the Canadian Broadcasting Corporation's English and Inuktitut Arctic service), Radio-Canada (CBC's French service), and an American station. Home Box Office, a private film channel, had been available for some time, but it was discontinued at the mayor's initiative, because it allegedly broadcast pornographic movies.

Almost all Quaqtamiut watch television regularly, although several adults state that their interest diminished since TV ceased to be a novelty. In many homes the television set is turned on all day long, but the sound is often cut off when the children are not there. English programming appears the most popular, because it is watched by everybody, even by the Inuktitut monolinguals. Programs such as 'All my Children' or 'Newhart' are particularly appreciated by Quaqtaq's older women, even if they do not understand English. The Inuit programs also attract a fairly large audience, but less so than the English ones.[37] Many bilingual Quaqtamiut find them comparatively dull, and prefer changing channels or turning their set off when they are aired. As for French television, it is occasionally watched by the youngsters schooled in the Oui-oui language, but English programs seem to be their preference.

Television is complemented by commercial videocassettes, available from two outlets in the village. These are invariably in English, and they are watched by a majority of residents, bilingual or not. A few private video recordings, mostly of a religious nature, are also in circulation.

In contrast to what is the case with television, where English predominates, radio is primarily an Inuktitut medium. All Quaqtamiut listen to the local radio station (*tusauti*: 'the listening instrument'), which broadcasts for seven hours a day and where local production (recorded music and community or personal announcements) alternates with programs from the CBC Arctic Quebec radio service (Inuit news and open lines). Inuktitut is spoken most of the time on the air, although the *tusauti* announcer may sometimes use English, for example, to introduce Qallunaat songs.

Outside the *tusauti* broadcasting hours, many Quaqtamiut listen to the Inuit programming on CBC radio. Some of them, a minority, are also interested in English-speaking information programs. Several state that they prefer radio broadcasts that 'tell a story' (i.e., are informative), to music or entertainment programs.

To sum up, the language situation in Quaqtaq may be characterized as one of diglossia.[38] The community now needs more than one language to function adequately. If Inuktitut still predominates when one has to deal with domestic and local matters, English and, to a lesser extent, French are indispensable for communicating with the outside. Even within the confines of the community, the Qallunaat languages are very present at school, in the homes of the non-Inuit residents, and every time a bilingual Quaqtamiuq needs to discuss or read about technology, administration, and national affairs in general.

In a way the most powerful of all languages now spoken in Quaqtaq is English, and this despite the fact that Inuktitut still appears as the predominant speech form. As in other Inuit villages, the Qallunaat tongue is the lingua franca (common idiom) of the community. With a very few exceptions,[39] it is the only language used by the local Qallunaat, whether francophone or anglophone, to communicate with the Inuit, because the vast majority of the bilingual Quaqtamiut have it as their second language. English also acts as the de facto official language. The deliberations of the municipal council and of several other administrative bodies are routinely translated into English (and not into French), and it is usually in English that the Quaqtaq representatives of most Inuit organizations communicate – at least in written form – with their headquarters. For things and concepts that have not yet received – or will never receive – an Inuit appellation, English words are generally used, and almost all children who learn French at school end up becoming Inuktitut–French–English trilinguals, whereas those whose second language is English remain bilingual.[40]

*Language Change*

This situation may explain why most Quaqtamiut feel that despite its predominance in the community, their language has undergone much change in recent decades. They often express this evolution by stating that Inuktitut is 'less strong' (*sungunnginirsaq*) than it used to be. This lack of strength appears to be particularly high among young people, but it also affects some adult and elderly individuals, whose pronunciation is thought to be deficient (*kutattut* 'they pronounce incorrectly'). Children, however, are said to speak Inuktitut better than adolescents and young adults, because they are partly schooled in this language. The best speakers are deemed to be a few middle-aged or elderly members of the community, both male and female,[41] who either belong to land-oriented families or work as teachers of Inuktitut. These people's speech is characterized by its rich vocabulary and, in some cases, its particularly clear pronunciation.

Inuktitut–English bilingualism is generally identified as the main cause for language change. It is true that most bilingual individuals tend to mix both languages. Some English words and expressions such as 'garbage,' 'juice,' 'telephone,' 'mom,' 'hey man' (a form of greeting), or 'see you' now belong to the everyday speech of the young and not-so-young Quaqtamiut. But other causes are at work. Many informants point to the fact that a great number of 'full Inuit words' (*uqausimmariit*) have disappeared from contemporary language, because their cultural referents have disappeared too. This results in a poorer vocabulary, whose users are unable to express some finer shades of thought. Others note that present-day speakers, particularly the youngest ones, tend to utter shortened words and sentences, using a smaller number of affixes and sometimes omitting the final part of lexemes.[42] Some also complain that Itivimiut (Hudson Bay coast) words have crept into the local speech. All these observations show that linguistic change is a complex phenomenon, which has been going on for a long time, and whose causes are multiple, including bilingualism, sociocultural transformations, and natural evolution of the language.

Thirty or forty years ago people were already complaining about the allegedly 'deficient language' of adolescents, often quoting examples similar to those that are still mentioned. Contact with the Qallunaat was often blamed for this situation, but language variation between the young and the old probably always has existed among the Inuit. Moreover, the Nunavik dialect as a whole has gradually evolved over the past two centuries, independently, as it seems, from any outside influence. Changes common to all Arctic Quebec speech forms include, for example, the gemination of consonant groupings (e.g., *uppik* instead of *ukpik* 'owl'), the law of double consonants (e.g., *aullatuq* in place of *aullartuq* 'he or she departs'), and the use of affixes without any initial wordbase (e.g., *-jjangittuq* 'it is not so'); for more details on this, see Dorais (1990, 1993).

When comparing their language with that of their neighbours, Quaqtamiut recognize that even if change is at work, it has not completely altered their way of speaking. They point out that linguistic problems may be more serious elsewhere. In large communities such as Kuujjuaq, for example, English is so widely spoken among the youngsters that, unlike their Quaqtaq peers, the young Kuujjuamiut often seem to have major difficulties with Inuktitut.[43] The native tongue thus remains stronger in Quaqtaq, even if it is not as strong as it once was.

When questioned about the specificity of their language, informants state that even if the Quaqtaq speech, like that of any other village, possesses its own peculiarities,[44] it does not constitute a separate dialect or subdialect. Quaqtamiut may say *aulasartut* ('they fish with a line') or *aupartuq* ('something red'), whereas their Kangirsuk neighbours prefer the words *iqiattatut* and *aupaluttaq*, or they may like to use affixes such as *-kallapaaluk* ('really a little bit'), *-paujaaluk* ('really looking much'), or *-lajumik* ('it means'), but this is not sufficient to characterize their language as different. The Quaqtaq people belong to the same linguistic community (*uqausiqatigiit* 'those who speak the same way') as the Kangiqsujuaq and Ungava coast Inuit. As stated by one informant, 'We understand all their words, whether they be short or long.' All of the word bases and affixes used in the Ungava linguistic community are fully intelligible to Quaqtamiut.

Within this community Quaqtamiut and Kangiqsujuamiut are deemed to be the people who speak the most correct Inuktitut (*kutannginirpaat*). Some older Quaqtamiut still distinguish between consonant groupings and geminates, pronouncing, for example, *ukpik* ('owl'), *aglapunga* ('I write'), *qingmiq* ('dog'), and *siniktuq* ('he or she sleeps'), instead of *uppik*, *allapunga*, *qimmiq*, and *sinittuq*. A very few occasionally use old plural forms such as *umiarjuit* ('ships') or *qilalukkat* ('belugas'), instead of the more regular *umiarjuat* and *qilalugait*. Most informants, though, admit that the Kangiqsujuaq speech is even purer than their own, because it is more complete (*uqarningit tatasimajurjuujartut* 'they seem to have a fuller speech'). In Kangiqsujuaq words are longer than in Quaqtaq (e.g., *nakuramik*, instead of *nakurmik* 'thank you'), because, it is thought, the Kangiqsujuamiut preserved their ancestors' language longer than elsewhere. In terms of linguistic modernity, Quaqtaq would thus occupy a sort of middle position between full conservatism and complete language change.

This position shows itself in the behaviour of many young Quaqtamiut women, who speak only Inuktitut to their children, but in a different way than their own mothers did. Crago, Annahatak, and Ningiuruvik (1993) found that the younger women were more apt than their elders to use question and answer forms, of a Euro-Canadian type, when interacting with their children. They also engaged them in more conversation with adults than used to be the case in Inuit families. Such behaviour helps young children to become fully articulate in the native language, and this at a very early age (see also Allen 1994).

*Language and Identity*

When questioned about the relative importance of their first and second languages, all Quaqtamiut answer that the knowledge and use of Inuktitut is indispensable to Inuit. For a majority of them, the native language is linked to their most basic identity. Typical statements on this topic (originally quoted in Dorais 1991: 23) include the following: 'The Inuit are characterized by their language' – 'If we lose our language, we will be like Qallunaat' – 'My thoughts and my heart can only be expressed through Inuit words.' Others insist that Inuit need Inuktitut because they feel more comfortable when speaking this language.

Some Quaqtamiut believe that even if the Nunavik residents are still fluent in Inuktitut, many of them – including several monolingual individuals

– think and act like Qallunaat. Some add that language is the only genuinely native cultural trait left to the Inuit, who otherwise have now lost their aboriginal way of life.

In spite of these statements about the importance of Inuktitut, everybody agrees on the need to know English and/or French. For most people, fluency in one or both of these languages is necessary if one wants to hold a decent job and survive adequately in the modern world.[45] Others stress that northern society has now become bilingual or trilingual, and that monolingualism or poor English/French fluency entails all kinds of practical problems.

Practicality is indeed the word. Quaqtamiut view the Qallunaat languages as the most suitable instruments for getting access to modernity. But at the same time, a majority state that Inuktitut must always come first and that English or French should only be learned as second or third languages. In the minds of most people there is a strong link between native language and identity. For example, two-thirds (twelve of eighteen) of my 1990 sample think that one cannot be labelled an *inutuinnaq* (a 'genuine Inuk') if one does not speak Inuktitut. Those six respondents who feel that one could be a 'genuine Inuk' even if one did not speak Inuktitut assert that language is of consequence, but that if one has Inuit parents, he or she will always remain an Inuk, even without knowledge of the language.

This last statement is important in that it puts into contrast two fundamentals of identity: kinship (genealogy) and language. It seems as if anybody born into an Inuit family would, by right of birth, retain a native identity. This would apply even if the individual in question did not speak Inuktitut or, presumably, did not abide by Inuit customs. Kinship relationships would thus have precedence over language as marker of identity.

Nevertheless, for most Quaqtamiut, an Inuk who cannot speak Inuktitut cannot be considered a real *inutuinnaq*. If, then, basic Inuit-ness is conferred by birth, the full development of an Inuit identity is unthinkable without some knowledge of the native language and culture. Fluency in Inuktitut, and an appreciation of Inuit culture, may confer a near-aboriginal status. For example, an Inuktitut-speaking Qallunaaq who socializes with local people will never become an Inuk, but in Quaqtaq, he or she will be identified as an *inuuqati* 'companion who lives the same life (as the Inuit).'

Kinship and language thus contribute much to the definition of who is, or is not, an Inuk. Together with religion, they bring a sense of continuity to a rapidly changing world. Their survival as important vectors of contemporary life shows that modernity can indeed be directly related to tradition.

# 5

# Quaqtaq and the World

In Quaqtaq, as in all other modern Inuit communities, native language and culture are constantly confronted by foreign ways of saying and doing things. The traditional *uqausiit* ('ways of speaking'; words) and *piusiit* ('ways of doing'; customs) are not adequate any more if one wants to interact with an outside world that is now within easy reach because of radio, television, telephone, fax machines, the Internet and frequent scheduled air service.[1]

In this chapter, I shall describe two phenomena that appear particularly important for understanding Quaqtaq's relations with the wider Canadian society: education and politics. First, however, we will see how Quaqtamiut conceptualize the relationship between their cultural identity and modern life in general.

## *Maqainniq* and *Kiinaujaliurutiit*

For most Quaqtamiut the various components of Inuit identity are subsumed into their connection with the land (*nuna*) and land-oriented activities. These last are generally referred to with words beginning with the base *maqait-* 'to be away': *maqaittuq* ('he or she is gone from home'), *maqaivvik* ('the place where one is away from home'), *maqainniq* ('the fact of being away'). Even if *maqait-* may apply to any type of travel, in Quaqtaq it has taken the specific meaning of 'being on the land,' in opposition to remaining in the village. The concept *maqainniq* thus epitomizes all of the hunting, fishing, gathering, trapping, and camping activities known to Quaqtamiut.

According to my informants, while people are at the *maqaivvik* (camp), they are more family oriented, traditional,[2] and religious than when they remain in the village. They also tend to speak more Inuktitut, English and French being irrelevant in such a context. At the *maqaivvik* too, individual problems are less prominent than in the settled community, because people live in harmony with their natural and social environment. Thus, *maqainniq* is perceived to be the most complete manifestation of Inuit identity. It is through *maqainniq* that one has the best chances to become, or remain, an *inutuinnaq*, a genuine Inuk. The prototypical *inutuinnait*, contemporary people's grandparents and great-grandparents, were able to draw their entire subsistence from *maqainniq* activities.

This type of identity, where one's position within the universe cannot be dissociated from his or her active relations with the community, the animals, and the material world, has been termed 'ecocentric' (Stairs 1992, Wenzel and Stairs 1988). One of the principal embodiments of an ecocentric identity is toponymy. Place-names create a 'memoryscape' (Nuttall 1992), a discourse that reminds people about how to use their territory and that evokes the mythical, historical, or personal events that occurred at these places. When travelling through – or speaking about – their land, Quaqtamiut are reminded, for example, that it includes good fishing spots (Iqaluppilik, 'where there are arctic char'; Tasirjuakuluk, 'the nice big lake'[3]), beluga and caribou hunting grounds (Qilalugarsiuvik, 'the place where beluga are hunted'; Nuliarvik, 'the place where they [the caribou] copulate'), suitable camping sites (Imilik, 'where there is fresh water'; Salliq, 'the flat island'), good travelling routes for sleds (Tuvaaluk, 'the big expanse of ice'). Names such as Illutalik ('where there is a house'), the home of the mythical Amautilialuk; Iggiajaq ('[the water passage] that looks like a throat'), the former winter camp and trading post; Airartuuq ('where *airait* are abundant'[4]), the famous hunting site, or Nuvuk ('the cape'), the abandoned site of the weather station, also convey memories that connect people with their individual or collective past, thus creating a sense of continuity and common identity.

In addition, the named landscape contributes to setting the Quaqtaq territory apart from neighbouring areas. Older Quaqtamiut know quite precisely which camps, hunting sites, and trapping grounds used to be visited by the Tuvaalummiut, and which were usually occupied by the Kangirsuk or Kangiqsujuaq people.[5] By granting well-defined rights of ownership and land use to Tuvaaluk Corporation, the local landholding body, the James Bay Agreement has formalized Quaqtaq's territorial specificity.

In the eyes of Quaqtamiut this specificity is the source of various cultural and behavioural characteristics that distinguish them from their neighbours. Because *maqainniq* still constitutes an important component of their lifestyle, and because Qallunaat reached their community later than some other parts of Nunavik, the Quaqtaq residents feel that they remain at the core of Inuit culture.[6] To quote a respondent, *maqainniq* is the basis of local culture; if it disappears Quaqtamiut will wander about without a goal. Many assert that the sharing of game has always been more developed in their community than elsewhere and that, even today, the sale of country food to the municipal freezer is not as important in Quaqtaq as it is elsewhere, because most of the catch is shared with family and friends. Kinship relations and mutual aid are allegedly stronger in Quaqtaq than in other places.

It is also thought that Quaqtamiut are sober in their speech. They do not talk when they have nothing to say, but when they do, they are not afraid to speak their minds. They are also deemed to work a lot. Women are particularly good at sewing, and Quaqtaq-made garments are renowned throughout Nunavik. Residents of other villages often buy skins and homemade parkas from Quaqtaq. Some consider this specialization an adaptation to winter, which is supposed to be longer in Tuvaaluk than elsewhere.

In spite of these characteristics that distinguish them from neighbouring communities, the Quaqtamiut stress that differences among villages are really minor. Some places (e.g., Kangiqsujuaq) are deemed a little more traditional than Quaqtaq, some a little less so, but on average, all Nunavik's hunting settlements share the same basic lifestyle. The former Killinirmiut, for example, assert that when they arrived in Quaqtaq they found no major difference from their home village, a fact that made their adaptation easier.

If *maqainniq* still stands at the core of Inuit – and Quaqtamiut – cultural identity, it is no longer sufficient to enable them to earn a decent living. In this modern world, employment has replaced hunting, fishing, and trapping as the main source of income. The concept of *pinasuk-* ('working'), which once referred primarily to those devoting their time to *uumajursiuniq* ('searching for animals'), *iqalunnianiq* ('going after fish'), *mikigiarnianiq* ('going out for traps'), and *mirsuniq* ('sewing'), is now almost exclusively used in connection with wage work. Economic success presently depends on one's abilities to perform on the labour market. Modern Inuit are thus compelled to know about what my informants call *kiinaujaliurutiit* ('means for making money'), the qualifications that enable people to find a suitable job.

The *kiinaujaliurutiit* do not stem from Inuit culture. They are introduced, taught, and controlled by Qallunaat. This is why the best place to learn them is the school, whose prime function appears to be the transmission of some useful means for making money. Because these means are basically Qallunaat affairs, the Qallunaat languages, English and French, stand among the most important *kiinaujaliurutiit*. Quaqtamiut deem that bilingualism and trilingualism have now become a necessity in the North. Most state that English and French are best learned in the classroom.[7] They thus consider it normal if the main teaching languages are those of the non-Inuit.

English and French, however, must retain their current status, that of mere second languages. This is why a majority of informants approve of Inuktitut being taught in school. If, however, classroom teaching can help with the preservation of the native language, it is not deemed sufficient. Parents and the community must make a special effort too, if they want their children to speak good Inuktitut. One older informant states that any able person can learn by himself or herself the words he or she needs. It is not by sitting all day long at a desk that a child will acquire a knowledge of Inuktitut. Other respondents mention the role of the church in preserving the native language.

Quaqtamiut are thus somewhat ambivalent about the *kiinaujaliurutiit*. They admit their necessity, but at the same time, they still value *maqainniq* highly. It is often said that the *inutuinnait*, those who fully practise *maqainniq*, respect their territory and do not spoil its resources, whereas Qallunaat 'wage war against the land' (*nunamik unatartut*). Several people add that most Inuit are now like Qallunaat, because their way of life is not much different from that of the majority of Canadians.

Such differences between Qallunaat and Inuit are readily discussed by Quaqtamiut, and they contribute to define the latter's position in the modern world. From a very tender age children are taught that there are two basic categories of people: their own (Inuit) and the other (Qallunaat). They are also made aware of the linguistic and cultural distinctions between those inhabitants of Quaqtaq who speak Inuktitut and socialize with Inuit, and those who do not. Children as young as 3 years of age may address an unknown Qallunaaq as '*Qallunaaq*,' thus hinting that they already discriminate on the basis of physical features. But I also observed older boys and girls who were surprised to learn that an Inuktitut-speaking Qallunaaq living in an Inuit home was not an Inuk.

My informants state that in addition to obvious features such as their language, clothes, hunting techniques, and physical appearance, Inuit are characterized by several behavioural traits that differentiate them from most Qallunaat. Some of these traits are considered positive: Inuit share what they have. They are extremely friendly, greeting each other in passing and doing a lot of visiting. Unlike Qallunaat, Inuit do not work just for money. Other traits, however, appear more negative: Inuit are deemed to be simple people, lacking intellectual curiosity; they are not really interested in inquiring about new ideas. They do not assert themselves as much as they should. This would explain why they need external aid to develop their territory.

Such an explanation remains very partial. The alleged lack of native development in the North is largely the result of two factors: (1) the parameters of development are generally defined by Southerners, who do not take into account the Inuit vision of economic, social, and cultural evolution; and (2) Inuit never had full control over the financial capital, political power, and technical knowledge necessary to foster southern-style development.

The main difference between Inuit and Qallunaat is linked to *maqainniq*. Because of their familiarity with the land and its resources, Arctic natives are able to manage by themselves everywhere in the North, whereas Qallunaat cannot survive without help from Inuit. The aboriginal population is thus the real master of its territory. For many Quaqtamiut this mastery is symbolized by country food, whose production proves that Inuit know how to use their own land, and whose consumption is perceived as one of the major distinctive characteristics of Arctic natives.[8]

When asked whether Inuit and Qallunaat can understand each other, half of my respondents answer no, and half utter a cautious yes: the two peoples need a lot of discussion and good will before the one can really know what the other is thinking. The problem with many Qallunaat is that they do not even realize that Inuit think differently from themselves.

Despite this alleged lack of understanding, however, most Quaqtamiut deem that Inuit and Qallunaat must help each other. For some informants, southern aid will be necessary as long as Inuit have not been trained to fill all locally available jobs. They state that they are thankful for Qallunaaq help, but that this is a transitory situation. In the long run, Inuit should be able to be completely autonomous.

Quaqtamiut perceive themselves as inextricably caught between *maqainniq*, the most basic expression of their Inuit identity, and *kiinaujaliurutiit*, the Qallunaaq-inspired means for earning a decent living. Many of them – perhaps the majority – think that *maqainniq* will eventually disappear, and that their grandchildren and great-grandchildren will lose their ancestral language and culture. But for the time being, most people seem willing to make a real effort to reconcile both aspects of life today and to define for themselves an identity that would be at the same time genuinely Inuit and totally modern.

## Education

Quaqtamiut consider formal education to be the principal vehicle for introducing *kiinaujaliurutiit* and, hence, modernity into the community. It is at school that the young are taught English, French, mathematics, science, and the other prerequisites for gaining access to the modern labour market. At the same time, however, most people think that the school can also play a useful part in the transmission of Inuktitut and of the traditional knowledge associated with *maqainniq*. Hence, the double and somewhat ambiguous nature of education as understood in Quaqtaq and other Arctic communities.[9]

### School as an Institution

Built in the mid-1980s, Quaqtaq's school (called Isummasaqvik, 'the place where one seeks to understand') stands out as the most impressive building in the village. It is also the biggest employer, with a staff of twelve to fourteen teachers and half a dozen administrative and maintenance personnel (see Chapter 3).

Because of the small number of pupils, the number of classes is limited. In the 1989–90 school year, for example, the sixty-seven students were distributed as follows:

Kindergarten (Inuktitut), 9 pupils
Grades 1–2 (Inuktitut), 11 pupils
Grades 3–4 (English), 9 pupils
Grades 5–6 (English), 10 pupils
Grades 3–6 (French), 8 pupils
Grades 7–9 (English), 7 pupils
Grades 7–9 (French), 13 pupils

The English and French classes were taught by Qallunaat teachers, except for one English elementary class that was taught by an Inuk. A Qallunaaq teacher was in charge of adult education, which mainly consisted in English as a second language, and two elders, a man and a woman, taught native skills. Inuktitut lessons were also available in the upper grades, but only on an occasional basis. All of the Inuit teachers were local residents.

In 1989–90 of all Quaqtaq students beyond Grade 2 55 per cent were in the English stream and 45 per cent in the French. These proportions may vary a lot from one year to another. In 1992–3, for example, a majority of parents decided to put their children in the French stream. As a general rule, most families tend to divide their school age youngsters between both streams, to maximize their linguistic knowledge.

Since 1991 Isummasaqvik School has extended its curriculum to Grade 10 (Secondary IV). The children are first taught to read, write, and count in Inuktitut (in both the syllabic and Roman orthographies), but from Grade 3 on, the principal teaching language becomes English or French. Although native culture (i.e., the *maqainniq* techniques, including hunting, sewing, and the knowledge of place-names), as well as religion and some grammar, continue to be taught in Inuktitut, the bulk of the curriculum is in the second language.

Beyond Grade 10 Quaqtamiut must go to Kuujjuaq to complete high school. Many are reluctant to do so, because they do not want to leave their families and community. Many parents, too, are unwilling to let their children go to Kuujjuaq, where personal and social problems are deemed to be much more severe than in Quaqtaq. This explains why the percentage of Quaqtamiut holding a high school diploma is very low. In 1991 (according to census data) of all Quaqtaq residents over 15 years of age, 59 per cent had not completed Grade 9, and only 23 per cent had graduated from high school. Some, however, manage to enter CEGEP (junior college). To do so, they must leave Nunavik and move to Montreal or its vicinity. A few Quaqtamiut have completed university studies, mainly in the field of teacher education.[10]

Isummasaqvik School is supervised by the local education committee, an elected body comprising five Quaqtaq residents. This committee instils a real measure of democracy into school administration, to the point that some teachers think it is too independent from Nunavik's central education authority, the Kativik School Board (KSB). According to them, the committee always has the last word over the board, often rejecting the results and recommendations of inquiries and evaluations conducted by KSB-hired experts.

Quaqtamiut generally appreciate the relative independence of their education committee. They even crave more autonomy, deploring, for example, that the present curriculum does not adequately reflect local and regional realities. In their opinion, KSB has yet to define a course of study that is not a translation or a copy of southern curricula, but stems from Inuit thought and knowledge. People would also like to see local history taught in the school. For them, culture and education should proceed from the immediate environment, rather than be imposed from above. Some Qallunaat teachers support these views. They state that formal education was forced on the Inuit and that, as a consequence, curricula and the whole organization of the school are like alien presences. Worked out by non-Inuit, they do not meet the real needs, wishes, and values of northern residents. This would explain why problems such as a low rate of academic success are recurrent.

At the same time, however, many Inuit parents complain that the school does not adequately prepare their children for the labour market. Students who move south find that they lag behind their peers of the same grade, and those who learn French are unable to communicate adequately in this language, because they mix it with English. School, as it now stands, is often deemed unable to teach marketable skills.

Such observations remain very partial. Formal education may be far from perfect,[11] but it alone cannot be blamed for northern unemployment. For geographical and historical reasons, the economy of the Arctic depends almost entirely on southern subsidies, and decent jobs will be hard to find, whatever the competencies of the northern residents, until this situation is rectified. What Quaqtamiut have to say about school is interesting, however, because it shows that, for them, education should clearly fill a double function: fostering and preserving local identity, on the one hand, and teaching young people how to earn a decent living, on the other.

*School Education and Community Education*

Another, related, dichotomy in the field of education is the contrast most Quaqtamiut perceive between traditional learning and the modern school. For them, Inuit education is – or was – a family or camp affair. Children learned by imitating their parents and other adults. When they were very young, they started participating in domestic and hunting–gathering tasks. Girls were thus introduced to sewing, fishing, cooking, and child care, while boys went hunting and trapping with their fathers. Special rituals celebrated the first accomplishments of the young people.

This type of education was based on example rather than words. Adults did not give much oral explanation, children being expected to learn through observation.[12] Young people thus acquired some knowledge about the *inuusiit* ('living habits'), the social and moral rules that govern community life, and about *pinasuarniq* ('working'), the various techniques linked to *maqainniq*. Education was thus geared towards the moulding of *inummariit* ('full individuals'), that is, socially and economically responsible adults able to survive the arctic environment. These adults were either male or female. Most informants state that with a few exceptions (e.g., girls brought up as boys) each child was educated according to the specific tasks he or she would have to perform as a grown-up man or woman. Some add that gender differences in education have now become obsolete, because both sexes should be able to perform the same tasks: *piqqajanngituliurniqariaqanngituq* ('there should not be any production of incompetent people').

In contrast to traditional education, school is seen as a place where one learns how to make money. Instead of *inuusiit* and *pinasuarniq*, school teaches some useful *kiinaujaliurutiit*. This teaching is conducted in a systematic way, and it relies on words. The teacher explains verbally what she or he seeks to transmit to children. Contrary to traditional learning, which required the active involvement of youngsters, school education is perceived as generating passivity: pupils just have to sit down and listen to their teacher.

For many Quaqtamiut, such passivity entails problems. When children had to learn by themselves, they were more autonomous than they now are, and they depended less on the external world. Those who did not go to school worked better than those who went. The extent of the children's knowledge, however, was rather low, but their overall morality was high because their parents forced them to abide by relatively severe regulations.

The biggest problem with modern school is that it tends to replace parents. Some people think that the blame lies with the parents themselves, who have declined to give any education to their kids. Others, however, see the situation as a confrontation between two different *piusiit* (customs): that of the government, which runs the school, and that of the Inuit. At home it is the parents who govern their children, but in the classroom it is the teacher. The pupils thus have to deal with two sets of *angajuqqaat* ('authorities') whose *piusiit* are often contradictory. For example, school hinders *maqainniq*, which is highly valued by most parents. As a consequence, parents are losing their leadership role. In the words of an informant, Inuit children used to dread their parents a lot (*angajuqqaaminik ilirasuttualuujaartut*), but now it is as if their ears were plugged when their father and mother are speaking.

Several middle-aged individuals consider this cleavage between young people and their elders to be the most important problem in the community.[13] In their opinion, many parents have given their children away to the school, and they cannot understand them any more. Parents used to show their children how to behave in life, but nowadays they do not teach them anything.[14] The school hires an *inuusiliriji* ('one who deals with the way of life') to give pupils some moral and social directions, but the results are far from conclusive. No wonder, then, that the two generations cannot understand each other.

Some people believe that this lack of communication is the source of current problems such as drugs and suicide. In their opinion, the ultimate culprit is the government. Because the federal and provincial authorities acted too rapidly and made decisions instead of the Inuit, the school became increasingly stronger and the parents compelled to forsake the education of their children. One's father's and mother's love and teachings cannot be replaced by anything else, and it is thus not surprising that problems are now so numerous.

Those who hold this opinion might be right, insofar as formal education was imposed on the Inuit without even asking them what they thought about it and how it should be adapted to their culture. But the cleavage between the school and the community, and the young and the old, encompasses much more than this simple dichotomy. Donna Patrick, a former adult educator in Quaqtaq, describes it as a dilemma between modernity and identity. This dilemma, within which the school is not entirely antagonistic to native identity, deals with 'making sense of young people's attraction to southern pop culture, their seeming economic need to master English or French and opportunity to pursue higher education only in the South, and their strong desire to maintain Inuit language and identity, as promoted in schools and in the values of the people I met' (Patrick 1994: 193).

*The Importance of Education*

Despite its potential problems and limitations, formal education is generally perceived by Quaqtamiut to be something positive and important. Most see it as an indispensable tool for understanding the world and for developing one's own thinking and attaining professional success.

Many others, however, put some restrictions on their overall appreciation of the school system. Some mention, for example, that education is useful if one gets a job after graduation, but that if schooling leads to unemployment, it would perhaps be preferable not to study at all. Others insist that all pupils should complete high school or even college, but because they have to go outside Quaqtaq or Nunavik to do so, they get involved in all kinds of problems, a fact that dampens their parents' enthusiasm for education.

A few people complain that some parents and children do not understand the real importance of formal learning. They give the example of students who attend school most of the year, but drop out just before exams. This alleged misunderstanding of the stakes of education might arise from the fact that in Quaqtaq, it would always be possible to find some kind of job without even having completed any schooling.

Several Quaqtamiut assert that formal education should not jeopardize the transmission of traditional *piusiit* (customs). For them, both types of knowledge are equally essential. A few informants even think that it would be better if Inuktitut were the only – or at least the principal – school language. More generally, all respondents state that going on the land fulfils an important educational function, because it is the best way to learn about nature, survival techniques, the Inuit language, and traditional values.

In Quaqtaq, then, education seems to serve a double purpose: (1) Education is meant to explain the contemporary world to young people and, it is hoped, help them acquire the skills necessary to earn a decent living in it. (2) Education is also perceived to be geared towards the transmission of what are deemed to be the traditional Inuit *piusiit, uqausiit* (words), moral values, and social customs.

As principal provider of *kiinaujaliurutiit* and systematic knowledge in general, school is seen as the main instrument for fulfilling the first function of education. But it also has a part to play in the transmission of Inuit matters, because most people consider it useful to the teaching of Inuktitut and of some traditional techniques. The main tools, however, for fulfilling the second function of education are family life and the *maqainniq* activities. Modern education thus seems to be perceived as a combination of both formal teaching and informal community instruction. It is this combination that ensures the preservation of local identity in the context of today's world.

## Politics

Quaqtamiut put a high value on their local culture and social customs. They also recognize, however, that their community is ruled by external laws adopted by various levels of government. Quaqtaq is a northern village within the province of Quebec, which is part of Canada. Its Inuit residents consider themselves to be aboriginal Quebeckers and Canadian citizens. They do not, however, identify themselves as Québécois, English or French Canadians, or, of course, Qallunaat.

Quaqtaq's administrative bodies were described in Chapter 3. The municipal council is answerable to the Kativik Regional Government (KRG), while the local education and social services committees operate under the respective aegis of the Kativik School Board (KSB) and of the Kativik Council on Health and Social Services (KCHSS). The three organizations must abide by the laws voted and implemented by the Quebec government, a power structure upon which the Inuit have no direct influence. Nunavik residents send deputies to Quebec's National Assembly and MPs to Canada's House of Commons, but their demographic weight is so insignificant in the ridings to which they belong, at both the provincial and federal levels, that during election campaigns candidates seldom bother to visit them. No Nunavik Inuk has ever been elected to the Quebec or Ottawa parliaments.[15]

KRG, KSB, and KCHSS, as well as the Makivik Corporation and other Inuit administrative bodies, are deemed useful by most Quaqtamiut. Their role is seen as one of guide and leader. They show the way to the local councils and committees, explain to them what looks problematic and put them into contact with the upper levels of government. The regional bodies, however, are expected to look at the local community organizations as their equals, and their interventions are resented when they seem too directive.

The small size of Quaqtaq is considered to be a hindrance to its autonomy. In the words of an informant, 'aulataujugut inukimut' ('we are manipulated because we are not numerous'). Several residents feel that they are not allowed to decide freely what is good for their community and that they must abide by the decisions taken by the regional bodies, even when they do not agree with them. Other people, however, think that these regional bodies have no autonomy of their own, and that some of them (e.g., the KRG) merely serve as transmission channels (aqqutiutuinnatut 'they are just routes') between government and the communities.[16]

In dealing with the federal and provincial power structure, Quaqtamiut must show solidarity with other Nunavik communities. On the question of hunting licences and game quotas, for example, all fourteen villages agreed on a common position, even if the Quaqtaq people felt that the deal was not completely fair to them.[17] This was the only way to have the regional opinion heard and respected by the governments.

Despite the fact that power ultimately lies in the hands of southern bureaucrats, many Quaqtamiut are thankful to Ottawa and Quebec for their alleged support of Inuit. They think that the role of both governments is to bring money, jobs, and education to northern residents. More specifically, the federal and provincial bureaucracies should help poorer people to earn a better living, by improving, among other things, their job training programs.

Because of Quebec's refusal, in the 1930s, to have anything to do with the welfare of its Inuit residents, the first, and, for a long time the only, provider of aid was the federal government. When the provincial authorities tried, in the 1960s and early 1970s, to gain control over the administration of Nunavik, the Inuit first showed some reservations. But after the James Bay Agreement they accepted that Quebec had now replaced Ottawa as the principal provider of services in the North. Loyalty to Canada remains strong, however. In the Quaqtaq municipal arena, for example, one finds two Canadian flags, but no Quebec *fleurdelisé*.

Over the past few years, Nunavik has entered a process of reexamining the administrative structures linked to the James Bay Agreeement. This process should lead to self-determination and some form of political autonomy. When asked about these questions, most Quaqtamiut remain very cautious. They generally favour self-determination, but are afraid that it might only turn into empty words. They point out that political autonomy consists in voting and implementing one's own laws and that to achieve that one must have full control over the necesary budgets. They wonder whether the southern governments will ever accept relinquishing some of their taxation and decision-making powers, to let the Inuit – and Nunavik residents, in general – do what they want in their own land.[18]

Some even question the desirability of self-determination. With three levels of government (federal, provincial, and self), would there be three income taxes to pay, or would one of the levels (either federal or provincial) disappear? Some informants state that the Kativik Regional Government (KRG) and the other administrative bodies are now under (*ataani*) the Quebec government, but that if KRG becomes autonomous, education and health care will pass under its direct supervision. The result might well be that new ways of doing things would have to be improvised, which could entail some degree of economic and social insecurity. The Inuit thus have to be cautious.

Caution must also be shown when it comes to Quebec's own political status. At the time of this research, the question of whether Quebec would become an autonomous part of Canada – or even an independent country – was not yet settled. The vast majority of Quaqtamiut – and other Nunavik natives – were against such an idea, because they felt it would sever their links with Canadian Inuit and isolate them completely.[19] A few, however, said that in any case they would remain in Nunavik and that the idea of independence could even be considered interesting if it permitted Quebec to develop in a better way and, thus, to help its northern citizens more efficiently.

Quaqtamiut realize that, politically speaking, they cannot escape external power, whether it stems from Ottawa, Quebec, or the Kativik Regional Government. But they are convinced that they are the only ones who really know what is good for them.[20] Ideally, then, the role of the various levels of government and administration should be to help them attain their own goals, rather than to give orders and take decisions on their behalf. Quaqtamiut admit the necessity of supralocal power, but they would wish this power to be fully receptive to their desiderata.

In Quaqtaq most people feel confident about their position in the world. They consider themselves to be specialists in the *maqainniq* activities and knowledgeable individuals capable of managing their own land. At the same time, they wish to master the available *kiinaujaliurutiit*, as well as technology and exogenous knowledge in general, perceiving no contradiction or discontinuity between tradition and modernity.

There is some fear, however, that young people might forget about *maqainniq*, without having it replaced by anything valuable. This is why Quaqtamiut put great confidence in education, provided it combines both formal school teaching and informal community instruction. It is the only way, they think, to preserve and transmit local identity, while ensuring at the same time the mastery of useful wage-earning techniques.

# Conclusion

The establishment and subsequent development of Quaqtaq resulted from the sedentarization of several families that used to move around in the Tuvaaluk (Diana Bay) area of northeastern Nunavik. Some of these families had always lived around Tuvaaluk. Some others came from neighbouring regions, although quite a few of these latter had originally been from the area.

Whatever their origin, these people came to Tuvaaluk and/or stayed there because game was plentiful. In the 1920s and 1930s they were also lured by the presence in the southern part of the bay (Iggiajaq) of trading posts that paid good prices for their furs. After 1940 various factors – including the proximity of the floe edge, the presence of a nearby weather station, and the establishment of a mission in 1947 – attracted most Tuvaalummiut towards Quaqtaq, which became the site of a permanent village around 1960.

Without ever becoming big Quaqtaq was progressively endowed with all the trappings of a modern community, such as prefabricated houses, a school, two churches, three stores, a post office, a radio station, an arena, and an airport. With the signing and implementation of the James Bay Agreement in the late 1970s, Quaqtaq's economic, political, and social life was reorganized on a more formal basis. The village became a municipality whose citizens had the opportunity to state their opinions – through various committees – on several issues, including hunting and fishing, education, and health and social services. The economy became more and more dependent on wage labour (*kiinaujaliurutiit*), although land activities (*maqainniq*) retained much prestige and cultural importance.

Modernity, as defined in the Introduction to this book, was thus seemingly at work in Quaqtaq. Local residents had lost control over their man-

agement of space and time, when dependence on traditional or semitradi-
tional seasonal cycles disappeared to be replaced by a wage economy and
southern-style patterns of residence. Formal education introduced exogenous habits and concepts, including several standard North American cultural symbols. One consequence of all this was that the Quaqtaq people
began to reflect about their own situation, often reaching conclusions at
variance with those put forward by the various official, Inuit and Qallunaat, organizations.

Through all these changes, however, Quaqtamiut preserved most of their
original values and social attitudes. The nomadic family bands of the pre-
trader era, which had become seasonal camp dwellers during, roughly, the
period extending between 1920 and 1960, survived within the modern cen-
tralized and institutionalized community under the form of kindreds, that
is, groups of families more closely related one to another – through blood,
adoption, marriage and name-giving – than they were to the rest of the
community. Together with the preservation of a privileged link with the
land, the daily use of Inuktitut, and some other factors, this survival
enabled the Quaqtaq people to maintain an ecocentric identity, that is, one
where a person's position within the universe cannot be dissociated from
his or her active relations with the community, nature, and the material
world. Economic, technical, and social change thus did not really affect
personal and cultural continuity between past and present, and this despite
the undeniable intrusion of modernity into the life of contemporary Inuit.

In such a context, the opposition between traditionalism and modernity
appears rather spurious. Many elements of material culture – notably all
those that were there before contact with Qallunaat – may be deemed 'traditional.' Similarly, a distinction can be made between 'traditional' and
'modern' institutions and social attitudes. Nevertheless, there is no clear-
cut dichotomy between the two. As we saw throughout the book, several
'traditional' values and ways of doing things have been carried over from
the past and still play a useful part in 'modern' life, albeit often in a modified form.

Among the 'traditional' phenomena still found in Quaqtaq is the presence of kindreds, which preserve a type of social organization, based on
family and kinship, that characterized the nomadic Inuit of old. Kindred
relations underlie, among other things, the marriage patterns (who marries
whom), name-giving habits, and church affiliation of present-day Quaqtamiut. In a sense, the kindreds contribute to maintaining social divisions
within the community. These divisions are, however, counterbalanced by
several 'modern' institutions that foster the emergence of a community

organization transcending the family and religious boundaries and that anybody may (and does) participate in, whatever his or her kindred affiliation. Such institutions, which help give all Quaqtamiut the sense of a common local identity, include the municipality (with its hockey arena and radio station), the school, the landholding corporation, and the cooperative.

To preserve the continuity of their social life and cultural identity, residents of Quaqtaq strive to conciliate the 'traditional' and 'modern' aspects of their existence, the *maqainniq* and the *kiinaujaliurutiit*. Among the principal phenomena within which this conciliation is operationalized are religion, language, and education. Religion maintains, under a Christian form, some very fundamental attitudes towards the natural and supranatural universe that have not changed much since the arrival of the missionaries. With regard to language, both Inuktitut and English or French are equally valued, but for different reasons: the former acts as a powerful agent of cultural identity, while the latter are perceived as indispensable tools for earning a better living and communicating with the rest of the world. Education is seen as encompassing both school teaching and community instruction, thus ensuring the simultaneous transmission of exogenous and indigenous knowledge.

As far as I can ascertain, most Quaqtamiut are able to integrate smoothly the various elements of their existence. Of course, problems do exist. Adolescents and young adults in particular seem particularly fragile, and their negative experiences with drugs, violence, and suicide are often blamed on accelerated modernization and cultural change. Nevertheless, on the whole, the community appears to work well, and the elders and middle-aged individuals still relate positively with the majority of the young people. When combining 'traditionalism' and 'modernity,' Quaqtaq residents do not give the impression that they think they 'live in two different worlds,' as some aboriginal people have said they do (see for instance, Kawagley 1995: vii). On the contrary, Quaqtamiut find it normal to try to get access to the best of the material, social, intellectual, and spiritual worlds, whether this best be deemed 'traditional' or 'modern.'

Quaqtamiut's self-perception appears to be generally positive. They see themselves as having preserved the core Inuit values in a better way than residents of many other northern communities. Several insist that in Quaqtaq income differences do not constitute a real problem. If, for example, somebody does not have the needed hunting and fishing implements (*maqaigutitsait* 'things that can be used for going on the land'), he or she may ask to accompany somebody else, thus obtaining access to the local resources. Work is greatly valued. If an able adult living in Quaqtaq is too lazy to produce anything, nobody will care about him or her. But if he or she is ambitious and works well, his or her social integration will be easy.

This situation, however, is perceived by many as being in jeopardy because of the overwhelming power of money, which renders *maqainniq* economically unattractive. For this reason the financial and logistical support of the various levels of government, and of Qallunaat in general, is deemed necessary for maintaining some degree of economic and social equality. In a somewhat paradoxical way, Qallunaat (and their institutions), who appear to most native Quaqtamiut as fundamentally different from themselves, may thus play an essential part in helping to maintain Inuit values and identity.

Important as they may be, however, these values will probably see their social and economic basis change over the next decades. A majority of Quaqtamiut think that within the near future, their village will grow in population, area, and business opportunities. But, at the same time, *maqainniq* will lose its importance, or even disappear completely. Some individuals, mainly in the older age groups, believe that this will toll the knell of 'traditional' culture. Inuit will become like Qallunaat, problems involving drugs and violence will increase tremendously, and homosexuality will appear. Most people, however, think that such a transformation would entail positive effects. Community residents would take their development into their own hands, and wage labour would be controlled by the local Inuit rather than by external agents. Quaqtaq could thus serve as example for other northern villages. The informants who express an opinion on their own personal future generally see themselves as working in some capacity for the benefit of their community, thus maintaining in a new context the basic Inuit values of mutual aid and solidarity.

Whatever the future may hold for them, present-day Quaqtamiut express a powerful aboriginal identity, coupled with a strong sense of belonging to their territory. When asked how they define themselves, people from all age groups generally answer that they are *inutuinnait* ('genuine Inuit') and/or *nunalituqait* ('old inhabitants of the land,' that is, members of a First Nation). Even if some respondents assert that modern Inuit are too much like Qallunaat to be called *inutuinnait*, the majority think that they still qualify for this appellation. Their sense of identity and belonging also shows up in their desire for a form of local autonomy that would enable them to decide for themselves, in respect of Nunavik's broader interests, how their community should be managed and developed.

One last question remains: Can one be, at the same time, Inuk and modern? The example of Quaqtaq – and, I believe, of most other Arctic communities – shows that the answer is an unqualified yes. Inuit live and work in fully modernized communities. Their identity is not to be found in a mere list of cultural attributes (e.g., igloos, shamans, hunting, and fishing). Inuit identity involves the specific way that Arctic natives establish their relationships with people, animals, the land, and the whole universe. Inuit feel continuity between their forebears and themselves, even when they are living in permanent communities, engaged in wage labour, attending school or local government meetings, or keeping records in Qallunaat languages. Genuine Inuit identity may thus find itself concomitantly in a 'traditional' as well as a 'modern' setting.

# Appendix A: Historical Events in Tuvaaluk and Quaqtaq, 1910–1990

1910    Establishment of a Révillon Frères trading station at Kangiqsujuaq (Wakeham Bay).

1914    Establishment of a Hudson's Bay Company (HBC) trading station at Kangiqsujuaq.

1921    Establishment of HBC and Révillon trading stations at Kangirsuk (Payne Bay).

1927    A free trader, Isumataaluk (Herbert Hall), opens a trading station at Iggiajaq (Diana Bay/Tuvaaluk).

1928    Establishment of a federal weather station at Nuvuk (Cape Hopes Advance).

1929    All Tuvaalummiut have now become Anglican Christians.

1932    Establishment of a Révillon trading station at Iggiajaq; Jean Berthé (Ijautialuuk) is the trader.

1936    The Révillon trading station at Iggiajaq becomes an HBC outpost.

1938    Berthé returns briefly to Iggiajaq as a free trader. He is accompanied by five Kangiqsujuaq families, those of Inuluk, Nua Masik, Nuvvukat, Miqquluk, and Tirtiluk. Isumataaluk dies and his store must close. Inuluk becomes manager of the HBC outpost.

1939    A trader named Cantley establishes a Baffin Trading Company (BTC) trading station at Iggiajaq. Taqulik becomes its manager.

1940    The HBC outpost at Iggiajaq closes. The Taqqiapik family moves from Tasiujaq to Tuvaaluk.

1941    The Nuvuk weather station operates during summer only. The Jaiku family moves from the Kuujjuaq area to Tuvaaluk. Inuluk and his family choose Quaqtaq as their winter camp.

1942    The Taqqiapik and Jaiku families choose Quaqtaq as their winter camp.

1945    The BTC trading station at Iggiajaq is managed by a Qallunaaq trader and the Nuvuk weather station operates all year long again.

1947    Umikallak (Father André Steinmann, OMI) establishes a Catholic mission at Quaqtaq and starts teaching school. The Inuit begin to receive family allowances from the federal government.

1949    The BTC trading station at Iggiajaq closes.

1952    Measles epidemics in Nunavik. Eleven people die at Tuvaaluk. The federal government starts paying attention to health care.

1959    Only one family spends the winter in a snowhouse. By fall, all Tuvaalummiut are living in wooden cabins.

1960    Establishment of a Federal Day School in Quaqtaq.

1961    The last two families to live in outlying camps, those of Maakusi Kiliutaq and Miaji Masik (Taqulik's widow), move to Quaqtaq.

1962    Three Quaqtaq families are persuaded by the federal government to move to Killiniq (Port Burwell).

1963    A Federal Nursing Station is built in Quaqtaq; it is visited from time to time by a Kuujjuaq nurse.

1964    Prefabricated houses are brought in by the federal government and sold (or rented) to the Quaqtaq people.

1965    An Inuit kayak is used for the last time in Tuvaaluk waters.

1966    The Quebec government opens a store in Quaqtaq. The village is linked to the outside by telephone. A consultative community council is elected. The use of snowmobiles becomes widespread.

1967    A provincial school is established in Quaqtaq. Scheduled mail and passenger air service links the village with Kuujjuaq. The Catholic mission closes.

1971    The Nuvuk weather station closes: it is moved to Quaqtaq, where local people take charge of it.

1972    A nurse lives in Quaqtaq all year round. Larger houses are built.

1973    The Quaqtaq store becomes a cooperative. Henry Angnatuk and his son George move from Killiniq to Quaqtaq.

1975    The James Bay Agreement entails the establishment of various local and regional organizations and committees.

1978    Education falls under the jurisdiction of the Kativik School Board, which builds a large school in Quaqtaq. A Pentecostal congregation is established in the village. After the closure of Killiniq, five families move from there to Quaqtaq.

1980    First election of a mayor and municipal councillors.

1981    The Quaqtaq cooperative is admitted into the Federation of Northern Quebec Cooperatives.

1983    The Quaqtamiut start receiving television.

1989    The airport and municipal arena are inaugurated.

# Appendix B: Adult Deaths in Tuvaaluk and Quaqtaq, 1941–1992

| Year of death | Name of the deceased | Age |
|---|---|---|
| 1941 | Sikuliaq | ? |
| 1942 | Inuguluaraq | ? |
| | Arpajuq | ? |
| | Uqittuq | ? |
| 1945 | Maaki Ittukutsuk | ? |
| | Inuluk | ? |
| 1947 | Saali Quiliq | 30 |
| 1948 | Alik Aggaajuuk | 45 |
| | Nua Masik | 45 |
| | Taqaq Liviina | 45 |
| 1949 | Marikallak | 32 |
| | Jupi Paaliaq | 35 |
| | Kasitiina Arjangajuk | 50 |
| 1950 | Pavvik | 26 |
| | Jaji Miqqualat | ? |
| | Harry Uvvaut | 60 |
| 1952 | Miqquluk | 35 |
| | Lisi Inugaluaq | 78 |
| | Maata Inuguluk | 48 |
| | Inugaluaq | 50 |
| | Nurraujaaluk | 60 |
| | Iiva Jaakkak | 43 |
| | Ilisapi Maqu | 52 |
| | Nurraujaq | 45 |
| | Nunalik | 55 |
| | Mini Qipalinnguaq | 40 |

| Year of death | Name of the deceased | Age |
|---|---|---|
| | Jaani Itigaittuq | 37 |
| | Taqqiapik | 60 |
| | Galakki | 30 |
| 1953 | Saaliti Kangilijjai | 29 |
| 1955 | Tiriganniaq | 36 |
| 1956 | Ripika | 25 |
| | Uiliaraq | 60 |
| 1959 | Samuili Ijjualuk | 60 |
| 1961 | Taqulik | 69 |
| | Jatsi Saquguluk | 48 |
| | Qarisaq | 52 |
| | Miaji Tirisi | 44 |
| 1963 | Maasiu Qalliutuuq | 42 |
| 1964 | Luisa Angugaujaq | 18 |
| 1965 | Qamuraaluk | 75 |
| 1966 | Lisi Arnaaraq | 75 |
| 1967 | Jaiku Napaaq | 64 |
| 1975 | Aalupa Itigaittuq | 45 |
| 1979 | Aani Anautaq | 60 |
| | Aani Inuppak | 65 |
| 1980 | Ikuagasaq Oovaut | 60 |
| 1981 | Henry Paaliaq Angnatuk | 70 |
| | Iiva Lisi Angnatuk | 44 |
| | Maaki Natsingajaq | 80 |
| 1982 | Lali Augiaq Tukkiapik | 62 |
| 1983 | Harry Kumak Oovaut | 51 |
| 1984 | Jaani Itiq Kauki | 69 |
| 1985 | Luisa Aloupa | 18 |
| | Iimali Jararusi | 70 |
| 1986 | Jupi Tukkiapik | 59 |
| | Putulialuk Pootoolik | 54 |
| 1988 | Ituaq Puttayuk | 61 |
| | Minialuk Oovaut | 74 |
| 1989 | Janice Deer | 17 |
| | Ilisapi Tukkiapik | 21 |
| 1990 | Willie Angnatuk | 61 |
| | Aqiggialuk Papak | 51 |
| | Maasiu Tukkiapik | 36 |
| 1992 | Miaji Siquaq Tukkiapik | 69 |
| | Iimali Qupanuaq Angnatuk | 78 |

# Appendix C: Peterhead Boats in Tuvaaluk, 1930–1967

### Sirli's (?–1937)
Bought in Kangiqsujuaq. Principally used at Inutsulaat by Sirli, his brother Kakiniq, his nephew Kangiimmaq, and Ijikittuq. Wrecked in 1937. Kakiniq died in the wreck. The boat was propelled by sail.

### Qungiaq's (1930–50)
Qungiaq bought this boat in Kuujjuaq. Besides its use by the owner, it was operated by Qungiaq's relatives Ikuagasaq, Jiimiaraq, and, more infrequently, Kuuttuq (Jiimi Koneak). After Qungiaq died in 1944, the boat was principally used by his brother Samuili. It was broken in 1950.

### Inuluk's and Nua's (1935–50)
Inuluk and Nua Masik, two brothers, bought this boat in Kangiqsujuaq around 1935. It arrived at Tuvaaluk (Iggiajaq) in 1938 (see Appendix A). It was operated by Inuluk, Nua Masik, Taqqiapik, Maasiu, Saali Tukkiapik, Sakkariasi, and, sometimes, Ituaq Puttayuk (Inuluk's son). In summer 1942 Inuluk brought the boat to Quaqtaq. After his death, in 1945, it was inherited by Taqqiapik. Taqqiapik was not related to Inuluk, but three of his children were to marry Inuluk's offspring, and one of his sons was named after him. The boat was wrecked around 1950.

### Nasaq's (1937–9)
It is unclear whether Nasaq had bought his boat in Kuujjuaq or Kangiqsujuaq. Whatever the case, he used it at Iggiajaq for about two years (1937–9), with his son Saami, Alik Aggaajuuk and Mususi. He then moved to Kangirsuk, where Saami was still operating the boat in 1966.

### Taqulik's (1937–61)
Because he had caught many foxes, Taqulik was able to buy this boat from

Isumataaluk in 1937. He operated it with Kaittaq, Tuukkaq, Jupi, and sometimes his brother, Maakusi Kiliutaq. After Taqulik died in 1961, the boat remained stranded on the beach in Quaqtaq. Maakusi Kiliutaq retrieved it in 1963 and sold it to Pita Airo, in Kangirsuk.

### Qaukkai's (1938)

Qaukkai and his boat spent about a year at Iggiajaq, in 1938, when Berthé (Ijautialuuk) briefly stayed there. The boat was operated by Qaukkai's sons Jaji and Jaani, and by Sakkariasi.

### Nuvvukat's (1938–51)

In 1938, or a little before, Nuvvukat bought this boat in Kangiqsujuaq, with some financial input from Miqquluk and Tirtiluk. The three co-owners moved to Tuvaaluk (Iggiajaq) with their families in 1938. Tirtiluk left for Kangirsuk a few months later, but the boat remained in Tuvaaluk, where it was operated by Miqquluk, Nunalik, and Matiusi Kululaaq. Because Nuvvukaat was often seasick, his use of the boat was limited. Nua Masik, who did not get along very well with his brother Inuluk, also used this boat. In 1950 Nuvvukat moved to Tasiujaq with the boat, which was wrecked in 1951.

### Jaiku's (1941)

Jaiku arrived from Kuujjuaq by boat in 1941, with his wife Lali, his mother Nammaajuq, and his mother-in-law Lusina. His boat had no motor and was propelled by sail. It was used around Iggiajaq during the summer (by Jaiku, his brother, Taqqiapik, and Taqqiapik's son, Saali), and then abandoned.

### Mission boat I (1950–5)

In 1950 Quaqtaq's Catholic mission received a boat for the missionary and the local Inuit. Everybody could travel and go hunting on this boat, but it was mainly operated by Saali Tukkiapik, Jugini, Ituaq Puttayuk, and Samuili, who was its skipper. The boat was wrecked in 1955.

### Mission boat II (1951–60)

In 1951 the Catholic mission was given a lifeboat by a passing ship. After having received a deck, it was lent to the local Inuit. Anybody without a boat could use it, but it was generally operated by Jajiapik, Taqqiapik (till he died in 1952), and his son, Maasiu. The boat was wrecked around 1960, with Jajiapik and Saali Tukkiapik on board.

### Maakusi's (1955–62)

Around 1955 Maakusi Kiliutaq and Papikattuq bought a boat that they operated themselves. When Maakusi left for Kangirsuk in 1962, he brought the boat with him. After having used it for a few months, he left it on the beach. The boat was sold to people from Tasiujaq in the summer of 1966.

### Mission boat III (Uppik's) (1956–65)

In 1956 Ituaq Puttayuk, Saali Tukkiapik, Miinnguq, Jugini, and Quaqtaq's Catholic missionary, Piratuan (Father Antoine, omi), went to Kuujjuaq in order to buy a new boat for the mission. Saali became its skipper. Between 1960 and 1964 the boat was generally operated by Saali Tukkiapik, Miinnguq, Aalupa, Putulik, and Ittuq. In September 1964 it was sold to Uppik, who operated it the following summer with his brother Saali Okpik, Aalupa, Miinnguq, and Tirtiluk. The boat was broken by ice in the fall of 1965.

### Matiusi's (1959–67)

In 1959 Quaqtaq's missionary was offered a lifeboat by a passing ship. He gave it to Putulik. When Putulik's father, Matiusi Kululaaq, came back from the hospital, he decked the boat (which was named *umiakajuk*) and together with his son, bought an inboard motor. Many people navigated on *umiakajuk*, but the most stable crew included Matiusi, his cousin Jaani, his son Putulik (when he was not employed at the Nuvuk weather station), Tuniq, and Miinnguq. The boat was abandoned in 1967.

### Ituaq's (1962–7)

In 1962 Ituaq Puttayuk came back from Resolution Island (Hudson Strait), where he had worked for the local weather station, with an old lifeboat that had once belonged to the Department of Transport. He decked it and bought a motor. The boat was generally operated by Ituaq, his brothers-in-law Saali and Jupi Tukkiapik, Itittuuq, and Ittuq. It was abandoned in 1967.

# Notes

## Introduction: On Modernity, Identity, and Quaqtaq

1 Anthropologists also define their practice in these terms, as they now distinguish 'modern' and 'postmodern' anthropology. To put it simply, the former would focus on hard explanatory theories (e.g., functionalism, structuralism, or Marxism), and the latter would try to replicate the culture-bearers' own discourse, without attempting to explain it. I prefer to consider myself a 'premodern' anthropologist, one who contents himself with a clear and, I hope, honest description of the people he is studying.

2 Many Quaqtamiut complain that since the advent of wage labour and the development of local and regional administrative bodies, it has become increasingly difficult to socialize properly, because people are always busy with work or meetings.

3 To give one example, traditional Inuktitut did not have any general word for 'work,' because hunting, sewing, or manufacturing implements were considered part of 'normal' life rather than as belonging to a specific category of activities. To express the modern concept of working, the Inuit thus had to coin lexemes approximating the Qallunaat idea: for example, *pinasuk-*, 'to strive to do something,' *iqqanaijaq-*, 'to be in the process of finishing something,' *suli-*, 'to do something.'

4 More properly, on the estuary of the Kangirsuk (Payne or Arnaud) River, which flows into Ungava Bay.

5 Edible berries include the black currant (*paurngaq*), gooseberry (*arpik*), and northern blueberry (*kigutanginnaq*).

6 Quaqtamiut call the island *Appatuuq* ('the one with a lot of murres'). Its official Inuit name, however (see Müller-Wille 1987), is *Arpatuq* ('the runner'), an obviously mistaken form imposed by northern bureaucrats, who did not care much about local usage.

7 On 18 June 1965, three killer whales (a male, a female, and a youngster) were spotted by a party of hunters, in a large opening in the Tuvaaluk floe, south of the village. The female and the youngster managed to escape, but the male was finally killed on 21 June. Spring 1965 is remembered by many Quaqtamiut as the 'spring of the killer whale.'

8 The caribou undergo demographic cycles of roughly sixty years, the causes of which are not completely clear. Traditional knowledge has transmitted memories of these demographic fluctuations, for instance, present-day Inuit often state that their great-grandparents had predicted that the caribou would return to their land some day.

9 Seagull eggs are also appreciated as food.

## Chapter 1  *Qallunaaqalaurtinagu*: When There Were No Qallunaat

1 All three populations share the same ancestors and a partly similar way of life. Their languages belong to the Eskaleut family (Dorais 1993).

2 Over several hundred years the artefacts found in Tuvaaluk's Dorset and Thule archeological sites preserve their respective specificity, in spite of the geographical proximity of the sites. After a period dated by archaeologists to about 500 years ago, however, no Dorset artefacts are found in Tuvaaluk.

3 The difference between the Dorset and Thule Eskimo languages was probably akin to the one that now distinguishes the more conservative Alaskan and Siberian Yupik speech forms from the more innovating Inuit dialects (see Dorais 1990).

4 These people are often referred to as *sivulivut* 'our predecessors,' and their culture as *sivulitta piusingit* 'our predecessors' customs.' See the title of Taamusi Qumaq's encyclopaedia about traditional life (Qumaq 1988): *Sivulitta piusitu- qangit* ('The ancient customs of our predecessors').

5 Several recordings and transcripts of interviews conducted in Quaqtaq by various people at different periods are deposited in the Montreal office of Avataq Cultural Institute, and/or at Université Laval, Quebec City.

6 They belonged to the families of Auqijauti, Nuvualiaq, and Naulikutaaq.

7 Those of Tiqqiingiq, Qisik, Uppik, and Siquaq (a widow).

8 Around 1900 the only two villages (i.e., places with permanent buildings and a year-round population) in Nunavik were the trading posts of Fort Chimo (Kuujjuaq) and Great Whale River (Kuujjuaraapik).

9 The snow house was heated and lighted by a seal-oil stone lamp that was also used to cook food.

10 In 1771 Haven had established the first Christian mission, which also operated as a trading post, among the Labrador Inuit at Nain. On the general history of the Canadian Inuit, see Crowe 1991.

11 Since, probably, the sixteenth century the Labrador natives traded metal and other goods with European fishermen on the Strait of Belle Isle and the north shore of the Gulf of Saint Lawrence.

12 Or at Great Whale River (Kuujjuaraapik), as far as the western Hudson Strait (Salluit and Ivujivik) Inuit are concerned.

## Chapter 2  The Formation of a Community

1 The station's permanent staff never exceeded three Qallunaat (two weathermen and a cook) and an Inuit family.

2 In the 1980 some younger Inuit, probably ignorant about this story – or feeling that the name of the place was not dignified enough –, asserted that Quaqtaq meant 'something frozen.' The story about Isumataaluk, though, was often confirmed to me by elders.

3 And, also, to leave it. The closing of the HBC store in 1940 seems to have been followed by the out-migration of some families, since the Tuvaaluk population of 1941 did not reach 100 individuals (compared with 105 residents in 1931).

4 They came from the Tasiujaq (Leaf Bay) and Kuujjuaq areas, but had already lived in Tuvaaluk during the 1920s.

5 Data found in this section owe much to information provided by Matiusi Kululaaq, Jiimi Kuuttuq (Koneak), Miaji Masik, and Miaji Taqqiapik, in 1965 and 1966.

6 This figure only includes the nineteen families who resided at one of the Tuvaaluk winter camps on 1 January 1943. It does not take into account those Kangirsuk families who summered at Airartuuq or Imilik in 1942.

7 A Catholic mission had been operating in Kangiqsujuaq since 1936. The establishment of Quaqtaq was part of a larger expansion movement of the Catholics in the eastern Arctic.

8 Almost all adults were already literate in syllabics, which they had learned from their parents and older siblings, or by themselves, going through their Bible and hymnal.

9 This particular year is used as a reference point because in February 1956 the anthropologist Bernard Saladin d'Anglure (Pirnaaluk) visited Tuvaaluk and compiled a nominative list of the population. I later completed his data by interviewing most of Quaqtaq's adults and elders and by consulting the Catholic mission's *Codex historicus* (daily diary) for this period.

10 That is, some three kilometres north of Quaqtaq. The Department of Transport forbade the Tuvaalummiut from settling at the weather station site, which explains why there was no camp at Nuvuk itself.

11 See Appendix C for brief historical sketches on the Tuvaaluk Peterhead boats and their crews.

12 For the three Iqaluppilik/Salliq families the preservation of a marginal migratory pattern can be partially explained by the fact that they did not have any close relatives – and only a very few distant ones – living in Quaqtaq at the time.

13 The Inuktitut appellation for them was *inulirijikkut* 'those who take care of the people.'

14 Upon hearing this, a Quaqtamiuq reportedly asked the NSO if he was up North to help the Inuit or not. If so, said he, the local Inuit should be left where they wanted to stay, namely, in the Quaqtaq area, where their ancestors had lived and died.

15 For a description of the early days of Quaqtaq as a settled village, see Currie 1963.

16 Data concerning this period come from my own field notes. I visited Quaqtaq in spring and summer 1965 and 1966 and at Christmas and New Year's in 1966–7.

17 Scheduled monthly or bimonthly airplane service to the Ungava Bay settlements started in January 1967 (the planes landed on skis or floats, depending on the season). It was supplemented by irregular flights chartered by one or another of the government agencies. Until 1967 such flights had been the only way to reach Quaqtaq (if one rules out boat, dog-team, and snowmobile travel).

18 Technically, a kindred is the sum of the individuals one recognizes as being his or her relatives. I use this word here to designate any group of individuals more closely related one to another – through blood, adoption, or marriage – than they are to the rest of the community.

19 Until fall 1966 the HBC store at Kangirsuk was the only place where the Quaqtamiut could sell the furs they had caught. After that, they also traded at the Quaqtaq provincial store, but because the HBC establishment was much better stocked, they continued to do some trading in Kangirsuk. In addition to seal, fox, and polar-bear skins, trading items included eider-down and walrus ivory.

20 For an excellent description of feminine activities in a small Nunavik village (Ivujivik), in 1965–6, see Guédon 1967.

21 In 1966–7, sixty-eight of the seventy-two Quaqtamiut were Anglican; the others belonged to the Catholic faith.

22 Or Notre-Dame de Koartac (Our Lady of Quaqtaq), the name officially adopted in 1961 by the Government of Quebec (see Brochu 1962). This name was later shortened to Koartac, when the provincial bureaucrats realized that it meant something like 'Our Lady of the Intestinal Worm.'

23 Two communities, Puvirnituq and Ivujivik, rejected the agreement on the ground that land was not for sale. They thus refused the new organizations it provided for (Rouland 1978).

24 After 1967 the DGNQ Kindergarten had expanded into a full-fledged elementary school.

25 At the same time, seven individuals moved out of Quaqtaq and four moved in; most of them were young men or women in search of a spouse.

26 This description is based on data collected during a short trip I made to Quaqtaq in July 1981.

27 These were three- or four-bedroom prefabricated wooden houses, with electricity and large water tanks (water was delivered by truck), but without showers or flush toilets.

28 When satellite television became available to Canada's Arctic communities, in the mid-1970s, the Nunavik Inuit organizations expressed strong opposition to it, because of television's alleged lack of northern content. This ban was lifted in 1983.

29 The Pentecostal religion had been introduced to the Canadian Arctic by Qallunaat preachers in the late 1960s and early 1970s.

## Chapter 3  Quaqtaq in the 1990s

1 Most of the data for this and the following chapters were gathered during two stays I made in Quaqtaq, in spring 1990 and winter 1993.

2 According to the Canadian census, fifty-five private dwellings were to be found in Quaqtaq in June 1991.

3 This station broadcasts within the limits of the village. Two-way CB radios are used for communicating with people travelling on the land or staying at outlying camps (Anonymous 1980). Incoming and outgoing phone calls – as well as television signals – are transmitted through a satellite antenna dish equipped with an automated transmission device.

4 In 1993, the former Catholic mission was still standing near the seashore. It was demolished two years later, to make place for a new nursing station.

5 And, for this reason, registered as beneficiaries of the James Bay Agreement.

6 These include five Qallunaat who settled in Quaqtaq between 1984 and 1988, to marry local girls.

7 Several babies also 'migrated' to or from Quaqtaq, when they were adopted or given into adoption by Quaqtamiut parents.

8 On 1 January 1991, twelve out of fifty households (24 per cent) bore the family name Tukkiapik (Taqqiapik). Other common surnames included Kulula (Kululaaq; six occurrences), Angnatuk (Arnatuq; six occurrences), and Oovaut (Uvvaut; four occurrences).

9 Some also hunt on Sunday, but this practice is generally considered to be contrary to religion.

10 These are large boats, longer than the Peterheads, hence their name.

11 In the absence of more accurate data, this amount was estimated by postulating

that family income in Quaqtaq should be more or less the same as the average of family incomes (as per the 1991 Canadian census) in three neighbouring and economically similar communities: Kangirsuk, Kangiqsujuaq, and Ivujivik. In addition to earnings from wage work and business, family income includes transfer payments (such as family allowances and old age pensions) and revenue from the sale of country products.

12 The gymnasium is often used for community-wide events: for example, Christ-mastime dance parties, sessions of the itinerant court of justice, and information meetings.

13 Secondary IV (Grade 10) was added in 1991.

14 It also operates a guest house where visitors who are staying a short time may rent a room.

## Chapter 4  Some Fundamentals of Identity

1 This assertiveness sometimes gives Quaqtamiut the reputation of being 'rough people' (as mentioned by several residents of a neighbouring village) or of con-sidering their community as 'the centre of the world,' to use the words of a local transient Qallunaaq. Nevertheless, Quaqtaq is also reputed as a 'warm and wel-coming community' (Séguin 1991).

2 Traditional Inuit names are not gender-specific. They may thus be borne by per-sons of both sexes. Christian names *are* gender-specific, but they are often used cross-sexually (a girl being named *Maasiu* – Matthew – for instance). In such cases, however, they will not be included among the principal names (e.g., those appearing on written documents) of the bearer.

3 Unsurprisingly, such 'modern' names are more common in mixed families. In 1990, for instance, the children of a French-Canadian man married to a local Inuk were named Natalie, Gabriel, Angelina, and Pierre; the son of a Quaqtaq resident born in Turkey was called Osman, and that of a Mohawk father had been given the name Sunchild.

4 In 1990, for instance, a Quaqtaq woman whose daughter had recently suffered a violent death asked that the name of this daughter be given to the yet unborn child of her son's girlfriend, if this child was to be a girl. The child was a girl. She was adopted by her grandmother, thus replacing her deceased aunt.

5 On 1 January 1991 only 14 of the 219 Inuit then residing in Quaqtaq where principally identified within the community by a traditional name (e.g., Putulik, Qupanuaq, Inugaluaq). With one exception (an 8-year-old child), all of them were over 30 years of age.

6 Saali and Jaji, the only two *sauniik* still alive, were, respectively, the boy's mater-nal grandfather and paternal great-uncle; Miaji had been his maternal grand-

mother, Maasiu his maternal uncle, Uili his paternal grandfather, and Putulialuk a non-kin whose relatives had asked that his name be revived.

7 Since the 1940s each Inuk person had received an identity number from the federal government. Carved on a pressed fibre disc (hence their name), these numbers were preceded by a prefix (E8 in Quaqtaq and the Ungava area) showing the region of origin of the individual.

8 Surnames between brackets are those of non-Inuit men married to local women and residing in Quaqtaq.

9 This percentage is similar to what has been found in other parts of the Arctic. In Igloolik, for instance, about 30 per cent of the Inuit population is adopted (Saladin d'Anglure 1992).

10 The members of these two kindreds married among themselves or, as has increasingly been the case, found a spouse in another community.

11 As mentioned in Chapter 2, Inuluk, who lived in Quaqtaq, and Nua Masik, from Iggiajaq, were brothers who had split residence as a result of misunderstandings. Thence the relations of cousinhood linking the members of Kindreds A and B.

12 Kindreds also exist in other communities of sedentarized hunter–gatherers. For an Innu (Montagnais) example, that of Sheshatshit (Northwest River, Labrador), see Mailhot 1993.

13 Data collected by the author during conversations with Quaqtaq hunters in 1966.

14 Interviews conducted by the author with eight men and ten women between 15 and 67 years of age.

15 Let us remember that on 1 January 1991, 102 (46.5 per cent) of Quaqtaq's 219 Inuit were children under 15 years of age.

16 Most transient Qallunaat reside in Quaqtaq for less than five years. There are a few exceptions though. In 1993, for instance, a female teacher had been returning to Quaqtaq, school year after school year, for over a decade.

17 The Inuit generally call such Qallunaat by their own names, whereas the others are addressed by their profession (e.g., 'teacher' or 'nurse'), or are not addressed at all. The practice of giving nicknames (e.g., Isumataaluk or Umikallak) to resident Qallunaat has almost completely disappeared.

18 Infants and young children are considered to belong to the same religion as their parents.

19 Only one all-Inuit household (from Kindred A) was religiously divided, the father being Anglican and the mother and children Pentecostal.

20 Parts of myths (the tale of Kaujjaajuk, the poor orphan boy, for instance), as well as stories about the shamans, are still remembered by some older Quaqtamiut, but despite their historical interest, they are not considered by them as relevant for explaining the modern world.

21 The 'antagonistic' point of view was that of the Qallunaat missionaries, whose interest it was to stress the discrepancies between the two religions (and, of course, the alleged inferiority and falsehood of shamanism), in order to make sure that the Inuit would make the 'right' choice, namely, Christianity.

22 One Quaqtaq elder witnessed one of these movements when living at Tasiujaq as a young man. The movement's followers (called *mumitsimajut* 'those who have turned over') used to walk around a tent in a counterclockwise direction, holding the back of each other's parka and singing hymns. In their prayers they had visions that they later reproduced on their clothes. On these movements, see Saladin d'Anglure 1984.

23 The first two were believed to dwell in the Tuvaaluk area (see Chapter 1). The third is (or was) sometimes seen swimming in the neighbouring waters. In the summer of 1966, I saw what appeared – because of the distance – as two black dots progressing one behind the other on the sea horizon. My Inuit companions suggested that this might be *lumaajuq* dragged along by the beluga she had harpooned, as told in the legend.

24 According to this woman, the person she saw was most probably an angel, or God Himself. It is interesting to note that she specifically mentioned that this supernatural being was a Qallunaaq. In her mind, it was probably unthinkable that God and His angels might look like Inuit.

25 In 1811 two Moravian missionaries, brothers Kohlmeister and Kmoch, had visited Kuujjuaq, followed, in 1872, 1880, and 1881, by three Catholics (fathers Arnaud, Lacasse, and Fafard). All of these visits were very brief and no conversions were attempted.

26 This rather unusual appellation, which originated in the Northwest Territories, might be because when the Catholic mass begins, the priest bends in front of the altar, his back turned on the congregation. In western Nunavik the Catholic missionaries are called *umiliit* ('the bearded ones') or *qaummaliit* ('those with robes').

27 One of them later preferred to attend the Pentecostal church.

28 Excerpt from a sermon delivered at the Quaqtaq Anglican church on Sunday, 7 March 1993.

29 Between 1981 and 1990 the growth of the Pentecostal congregation was attributable to the numerous members of Kindred C and, to a lesser extent, Kindred A, who joined the Four Gospels church.

30 Pentecostal members of Kindred A are either married to a Pentecostal from Kindred C or belong to one particular family, genealogically marginal within Kindred A, whose members and their spouses, with one exception, joined the Four Gospels church around 1985.

31 Excerpt from an interview with a Pentecostal woman, Quaqtaq, June 1990.

32 Another service is held in late afternoon. It also happens that the preacher and

his wife visit the homes of those unable to attend church, in order to pray with them.

33 This man is deeply interested in religious matters. In the late 1980s he even visited Jerusalem, thanks to the financial support of a Qallunaaq friend. His preaching is entirely conducted in Inuktitut.

34 The Four Gospels church is thus officially recognized as a bona fide religious organization. In 1993, though, it was not yet allowed to legalize marriages, and people had to make their union official at the Anglican church.

35 Such attitudes, quite similar to the modern Anglo-Saxon work ethic, may stem from the fact that Pentecostalism was originally born in the United States as a religious expression and justification of the most basic values of American capitalism.

36 One of these learned English from the Catholic missionaries, in exchange for Inuktitut lessons. He also spent a few years in a southern hospital. The other was sent to Toronto for medical care when a young man and lived there for about ten years.

37 In 1990 a weekly total of about twenty to twenty-five hours of Inuktitut television was available on CBC North. It mainly consisted in reporting on northern political, arts, or sports events, or in hunting or travel stories told by middle-aged or elderly people.

38 Diglossia is defined as a situation where a population needs two or more languages – of unequal status – to perform all the tasks needed to ensure its collective survival. On diglossia in the Canadian Arctic, see Dorais 1989.

39 One major exception is school, where the French teachers always address their pupils in this language. For a description of the language situation in a larger Nunavik community, see Taylor and Wright 1989.

40 A similar situation has been observed in other Nunavik communities (see Patrick 1994).

41 The Quaqtamiut do not perceive any difference in the speech of men and women, except that traditionally each sex knew better than the other the technical vocabulary linked to his or her specific tasks.

42 An oft-quoted example is *pitaqanngi-*, instead of *pitaqanngituq* ('there is not').

43 For instance, young Kuujjuamiut (and, also, a very few Quaqtaq youngsters) do not use the dual any more (e.g., *saimulaurta* rather than *saimulaurluk* 'let's [both of us] shake hands'), or they utter forms such as *pilaurlara* 'may I get it,' in place of the grammatically correct *pilaurlagu*. My Quaqtaq informants note, though, that the language of the adult Kuujjuamiut is similar to their own.

44 For instance, it would sound less musical than that of other communities.

45 When asked about the relative importance of English in relation to French, a majority of informants state that the former language is more useful than the latter, but that ideally, the young Inuit should know both.

## Chapter 5 Quaqtaq and the World

1 In 1993 there were at least four flights a week between Quaqtaq, Kuujjuaq, and the neighbouring communities. Daily flights linked Kuujjuaq with southern Canada.

2 In the sense that they abide more completely by Inuit customs (*piusiit*), for example, hunting and fishing for subsistence, eating country food, and sharing and helping each other.

3 The word *tasiq* 'lake' applies only to an expanse of freshwater teeming with fish. Thus, *tasirjuakuluk* actually means 'the nice big place with fish.'

4 Airartuuq is not named for its abundance of sea mammals, however, but for an insignificant resource, the *airaq,* a small edible root.

5 They also consider some sites such as Tasirjuakuluk or Imilik, to be mixed Quaqtaq – Kangirsuk territories.

6 According to an informant, this core is like the earth's nucleus: it is still hot but increasingly cooling off, because of the influence of foreign words, customs, and ideas.

7 Some add, however, that school is not sufficient. To become really fluent one has to work on a daily basis with anglophones or francophones.

8 Genuine Inuit foods include *aulik* ('[raw] meat with its blood') and *igunaq* ('gamy meat').

9 Interviews I administered in Igloolik (Baffin Region) in 1991 showed a similar opinion about the school, which was perceived both as agent of modernity and as potential tool for preserving Inuit language and culture (on this topic, see Dorais 1995).

10 Teacher training is offered by the Kativik School Board, under the supervision of McGill University. Lack of extended formal education often hinders post-secondary studies. One Quaqtaq man, for instance, who had been accepted to study journalism in a southern university, had to quit after a few months when he realized that, with his Grade 9 education, he would have had to study day and night to cope with the requirements of his program.

11 For one thing, it *is* alien, being principally conducted in languages that are not those of the local population.

12 Some skills could even be learned individually. Syllabic literacy, for instance, was often acquired by browsing through the Bible without outside support or with the help of one's siblings.

13 Both Inuit and Qallunaat with whom I discussed this topic stated their opinion in almost similar words.

14 Some parents are also deemed to be somewhat mixed up in their thoughts and identity. For example, they consider Inuit culture and history to be dull and use-less, and they do not wish to transmit these to their children.

15 In this the situation of the Quebec Inuit is different from that of the Northwest Territories natives, who send aboriginal deputies to Yellowknife and Ottawa.

16 I agree with this opinion, because the powers of decision of KRG are strictly limited by Quebec law. It is interesting to note that in French, KRG is called Administration régionale Kativik. It is thus defined as a purely administrative body rather than as a government, as its English (Kativik Regional Government) and Inuktitut (Kativik nunalilimaat kavamangat, 'Kativik, the government of all villages') names might lead one to believe.

17 More specifically, they thought that their quota of beluga whales could have been higher, without jeopardizing the survival of the herds.

18 I cannot but agree with such an opinion, which is consistent with the fact that most present-day organizations are perceived as mere driving belts for implementing decisions taken outside Nunavik.

19 A Nunavik-wide consultation on Quebec's sovereignty, organized by the Makivik Corporation shortly before the provincial referendum of 30 October 1995 (which rejected independence by a margin of less than 1 per cent), yielded very clear results: more than 95 per cent of the Quebec Inuit voted against sovereignty.

20 When discussing this topic, one is always reminded that in the early 1960s the federal government wished to close Quaqtaq, but that the village remained alive thanks to its inhabitants' refusal to move anywhere else (see Chapter 2).

# References

Alia, Valerie. 1994. *Names, Numbers, and Northern Policy: Inuit, Project Surname, and the Politics of Identity.* Halifax: Fernwood Publishing.

Allen, Shanley E.M. 1994. 'Acquisition of Some Mechanisms of Transitivity Alternation in Arctic Quebec Inuktitut.' PhD dissertation, McGill University, Montreal.

Anonymous. 1980. 'Tests with Field Radios in Koartak.' *Inuktitut*, November: 45–9.

Arcand, Bernard. 1993. *The Jaguar and the Anteater: Pornography and the Modern World.* Toronto: McClelland and Stewart.

Badgley, Ian. 1980. 'Stratigraphy and Habitation Features at DIA.4 (JfEl-4), a Dorset Site in Arctic Québec.' *Arctic*, 33(3): 569–84.

Barth, Fredrik. 1969. 'Introduction,' in *Ethnic Groups and Boundaries*, ed. F. Barth. Boston: Little, Brown, 9–38.

Bibeau, P. 1984. *Établissements paléoesquimaux du site Diana 73, Ungava.* Montréal: Université du Québec à Montréal (Paléo-Québec No. 16).

Brochu, Michel. 1962. *Le défi du Nouveau-Québec.* Montréal: Éditions du Jour.

Camilleri, Carmel, ed. 1990. *Stratégies identitaires.* Paris: Presses Universitaires de France.

Collin, Dominique. 1991. 'Identité amérindienne et inuit moderne.' PhD dissertation, Université de Montréal.

Crago, Martha B., Betsy Annahatak, and Lizzie Ningiuruvik. 1993. 'Changing Patterns of Language Socialization in Inuit Homes.' *Anthropology and Education Quarterly*, 24(3): 205–23.

Crowe, Keith J. 1979. 'A Summary of Northern Native Claims in Canada: The Process and Progress of Negotiations.' *Études/Inuit/Studies*, 3(1): 31–9.

– 1991. *A History of the Original Peoples of Northern Canada*, 2nd ed. Montreal: McGill-Queen's University Press.

128    References

Currie, R.D. 1963. *Western Ungava Area Economic Survey*. Ottawa: Department of Northern Affairs.

Dawson, B., 1984. 'The Expulsion of the Killiniq Inuit.' *Taqralik,* February: 42–6.

Dorais, Louis-Jacques. 1979. 'The Dynamics of Contact between French Nationalism and Inuktitut in Northern Quebec,' in *Eskimo Languages*, ed. B. Basse and K. Jensen. Aarhus: Arkona, 69–76.

– 1984. *Les Tuvaalummiut: Histoire sociale des Inuit de Quaqtaq (Québec arctique)*. Montréal: Recherches amérindiennes au Québec (Signes des Amériques, 4).

– 1985. 'Un sauvage chez le vrai monde,' in *La passion de l'échange: Terrains d'anthropologues du Québec*, ed. S. Genest. Chicoutimi: Gaétan Morin Éditeur, 85–99.

– 1988. 'Inuit Identity in Canada.' *Folk*, 30: 23–31.

– 1989. 'Bilingualism and Diglossia in the Canadian Eastern Arctic.' *Arctic*, 42(3): 199–207.

– 1990. *Inuit uqausiqatigiit: Inuit Languages and Dialects*. Iqaluit: Arctic College.

– 1991. 'Language, Identity and Integration in the Canadian Arctic.' *North Atlantic Studies,* 3(1): 18–24.

– 1993. *From Magic Words to Word Processing: A History of the Inuit Language*. Iqaluit: Arctic College.

– 1995. 'Language, Culture and Identity: Some Inuit Examples.' *Canadian Journal of Native Studies*, 15(2): 293–308.

– and Bernard Saladin d'Anglure, 1988. 'Roman Catholic Missions in the Arctic,' in *Handbook of North American Indians, vol. 4: History of Indian-White Relations*, ed. W.E. Washburn. Washington: Smithsonian Institution, 501–5.

Duhaime, Gérard. 1990. 'Programme d'aide aux Inuit: Tradition et modernité.' *Recherches sociographiques*, 31(1): 45–62.

Giddens, Anthony. 1991. *Modernity and Self-Identity*. Palo Alto: Stanford University Press.

Graburn, Nelson H.H. 1969. *Eskimos without Igloos*. Boston: Little Brown.

Guédon, Marie-Françoise. 1967. 'Organisation des activités féminines dans la communauté esquimaude d'Ivujivik (Nouveau-Québec).' Thèse de maîtrise en anthropologie, Université de Montréal.

Hawkes, Edward W. 1916. *The Labrador Eskimo*. Ottawa: Department of Mines, Geological Survey (memoir 91).

Helm, June. 1965. 'Bilaterality in the Socio-Territorial Organization of the Arctic Drainage Dene.' *Ethnology*, 4(4): 361–85.

Jacobson-Widding, Anita, ed. 1983. *Identity: Personal and Socio-Cultural*. Uppsala: Almquist-Wiksell.

Jenness, Diamond. 1964. *Eskimo Administration: II. Canada*. Montreal: Arctic Institute of North America (Technical Paper No. 14).

Julien, M. 1980. 'Étude préliminaire du matériel osseux provenant du site dorsétien DIA.4 (JfEl-4) (Arctique oriental).' *Arctic,* 33(3): 553–68.

Kativik Regional Government (KRG). 1980. *Technical Analysis of Inuit Involvement Through Job Opportunities in the 13 Municipalities North of the 55th Parallel.* Kuujjuaq: Kativik Regional Government.

Kawagley, Angayuqaq Oscar. 1995. *A Yupiaq Worldview.* Prospect Heights: Waveland Press.

Kirmayer, Laurence J., Chris. Fletcher, Ellen Corin, and L. Boothroyd. 1994. *Inuit Concepts of Mental Health and Illness: An Ethnographic Study.* Montreal: Sir Mortimer B. Davis–Jewish General Hospital, Institute of Community and Family Psychiatry.

Lee, Thomas. 1979. 'Norse in Ungava.' *Anthropological Journal of Canada,* 17(1): 2–31 and 17(2): 2–43.

Low, Albert P. 1906. *The Cruise of the Neptune.* Ottawa: Government of Canada.

Lynge, Finn. 1992. *Arctic Wars, Animal Rights, Endangered Peoples.* Hanover: University Press of New England.

Mailhot, Jose. 1993. *Au pays des Innus: Les gens de Sheshatshit.* Montréal: Recherches amérindiennes au Québec.

Ministère des institutions financières et des corporations (MIFC). 1981. *Évaluation des revenus et des dépenses de la population autochtone des 13 municipalités du Nouveau-Québec.* Québec: Gouvernement du Québec.

Müller-Wille, Ludger. 1987. *Inuttitut Nunait atingit Katirsutauningit Nunavimi (Kupaimmi, Kanatami): Gazetteer of Inuit Place Names in Nunavik (Québec, Canada). Répertoire toponymique inuit du Nunavik (Québec, Canada).* Inukjuak: Avataq Cultural Institute.

Nuttall, Mark. 1992. *Arctic Homeland: Kinship, Community and Development in Northwest Greenland.* Toronto: University of Toronto Press.

Patrick, Donna. 1994. 'Minority Language Education and Social Context.' *Études/Inuit/Studies,* 18(1–2): 183–99.

Payne, F.F. 1899. 'Eskimo of Hudson's Strait.' *Proceedings of the Canadian Institute,* 3(VI): 213–30.

Plumet, Patrick. 1978. 'Le Nouveau-Québec et le Labrador,' in *Images de la préhistoire du Québec,* ed. Claude Chapdelaine. Montréal: Recherches amérindiennes au Québec, 99–110.

– 1985. *Archéologie de l'Ungava: Le site de la Pointe aux Bélougas (Qilalugarsiuvik) et les maisons longues dorsétiennes.* Montréal: Université du Québec à Montréal (Paléo-Québec No. 18).

Plumet, Patrick, and Ian Badgley. 1980. 'Implications méthodologiques des fouilles de Tuvaaluk sur l'étude des établissements dorsétiens.' *Arctic,* 33(3): 542–52.

Qumaq, Taamusi. 1988. *Sivulitta piusituqangit.* Québec: Association Inuksiutiit Katimajiit (Inuksiutiit Allaniagait 5).

Rouland, Norbert. 1978. *Les Inuit du Nouveau-Québec et la Convention de la Baie James.* Québec: Association Inuksiutiit Katimajiit et Centre d'études nordiques de l'Université Laval.

Saladin d'Anglure, Bernard. 1967. *L'organisation sociale traditionnelle des Esquimaux de Kangirsujuaaq (Nouveau-Québec).* Québec: Université Laval, Centre d'études nordiques.

– 1984. 'Inuit of Quebec,' in *Handbook of North American Indians, vol. 5, Arctic,* ed. D. Damas. Washington: Smithsonian Institution, 476–507.

– 1992. 'Le "troisième" sexe.' *La Recherche,* 245: 836–44.

Séguin, Louise. 1991. 'Quaqtaq, between the Sky and the Sea.' *Rencontre,* 13(2): 12–14.

Stairs, Arlene. 1990. 'Questions behind the Question of Vernacular Education: A Study in Literacy, Native Language and English.' *English Quarterly,* 22: 103–24.

– 1992. 'Self-Image, World-Image: Speculations on Identity from Experiences with Inuit.' *Ethos,* 20(1): 116–26.

Steinmann, André. 1977. *La petite barbe.* Montréal: Éditions de l'Homme.

Taylor, Donald M., and S.C. Wright. 1989. 'Language Attitudes in a Multilingual Northern Community.' *Canadian Journal of Native Studies,* 9(1): 85–119.

Taylor, J. Garth. 1975. 'Demography and Adaptation of Eighteenth-Century Eskimo Groups in Northern Labrador and Ungava,' in *Prehistoric Maritime Adaptations of the Circumpolar Zone,* ed. W. Fitzhugh. The Hague: Mouton, 269–78.

Turner, Lucien M. 1979 (1894). *Indians and Eskimos in the Quebec-Labrador Peninsula.* Québec: Inuksiutiit Association and Presses Comeditex (reprint of the original edition, Smithsonian Institution, Washington).

Vézinet, Monique. 1980. *Les Nunamiut, Inuit au coeur des terres.* Québec: Éditeur officiel.

– 1982. *Occupation humaine de l'Ungava: Perspective ethno-historique et écologique.* Montréal: Université du Québec à Montréal (Paléo-Québec No. 14).

Wenzel, George, and Arlene Stairs. 1988. 'I am I and the Environment: Inuit Hunting, Community, and Identity.' Unpublished ms., Department of Geography, McGill University, Montreal.

# Index